ASI 8661   2

Children's Literature

THE GREENHAVEN PRESS COMPANION TO
Literary Movements and Genres

Children's Literature

Wendy Mass, *Book Editor*

David L. Bender, *Publisher*

Bruno Leone, *Executive Editor*

Bonnie Szumski, *Editorial Director*

Stuart B. Miller, *Managing Editor*

David M. Haugen, *Series Editor*

Greenhaven Press, Inc., San Diego, CA

Every effort has been made to trace the owners of copyrighted material. The articles in this volume may have been edited for content, length, and/or reading level. The titles have been changed to enhance the editorial purpose. Those interested in locating the original source will find the complete citation on the first page of each article.

Library of Congress Cataloging-in-Publication Data

Children's literature / Wendy Mass, book editor.
     p.   cm. — (Literary movements and genres)
   Includes bibliographical references and index.
   ISBN 0-7377-0567-1 (pbk. : alk. paper) —
ISBN 0-7377-0568-X (lib. : alk. paper)
   1. Children's literature, English—History and criticism. 2. Children's literature, American—History and criticism. 3. Children—Books and reading. I. Mass, Wendy, 1967– . II. Series.

PR990 .C494 2001
820.9'9282—dc21   00-056049
                                     CIP

Cover photo: Christie's Images, London/Bridgeman Art Library, London/Superstock
Library of Congress, 16, 62, 84, 102, 124

Copyright © 2001 by Greenhaven Press, Inc.
PO Box 289009
San Diego, CA 92198-9009
Printed in the U.S.A.

CONTENTS

Chapter 4: Controversy in Children's Literature

FOREWORD

The study of literature most often involves focusing on an individual work and uncovering its themes, stylistic conventions, and historical relevance. It is also enlightening to examine multiple works by a single author, identifying similarities and differences among texts and tracing the author's development as an artist.

While the study of individual works and authors is instructive, however, examining groups of authors who shared certain cultural or historical experiences adds a further richness to the study of literature. By focusing on literary movements and genres, readers gain a greater appreciation of influence of historical events and social circumstances on the development of particular literary forms and themes. For example, in the early twentieth century, rapid technological and industrial advances, mass urban migration, World War I, and other events contributed to the emergence of a movement known as American modernism. The dramatic social changes, and the uncertainty they created, were reflected in an increased use of free verse in poetry, the stream-of-consciousness technique in fiction, and a general sense of historical discontinuity and crisis of faith in most of the literature of the era. By focusing on these commonalities, readers attain a more comprehensive picture of the complex interplay of social, economic, political, aesthetic, and philosophical forces and ideas that create the tenor of any era. In the nineteenth-century American romanticism movement, for example, authors shared many ideas concerning the preeminence of the self-reliant individual, the infusion of nature with spiritual significance, and the potential of persons to achieve transcendence via communion with nature. However, despite their commonalities, American romantics often differed significantly in their thematic and stylistic approaches. Walt Whitman celebrated the communal nature of America's open democratic society, while Ralph Waldo

Emerson expressed the need for individuals to pursue their own fulfillment regardless of their fellow citizens. Herman Melville wrote novels in a largely naturalistic style whereas Nathaniel Hawthorne's novels were gothic and allegorical.

Another valuable reason to investigate literary movements and genres lies in their potential to clarify the process of literary evolution. By examining groups of authors, literary trends across time become evident. The reader learns, for instance, how English romanticism was transformed as it crossed the Atlantic to America. The poetry of Lord Byron, William Wordsworth, and John Keats celebrated the restorative potential of rural scenes. The American romantics, writing later in the century, shared their English counterparts' faith in nature; but American authors were more likely to present an ambiguous view of nature as a source of liberation as well as the dwelling place of personal demons. The whale in Melville's *Moby-Dick* and the forests in Hawthorne's novels and stories bear little resemblance to the benign pastoral scenes in Wordsworth's lyric poems.

Each volume in Greenhaven Press's Companions to Literary Movements and Genres series begins with an introductory essay that places the topic in a historical and literary context. The essays that follow are carefully chosen and edited for ease of comprehension. These essays are arranged into clearly defined chapters that are outlined in a concise annotated table of contents. Finally, a thorough chronology maps out crucial literary milestones of the movement or genre as well as significant social and historical events. Readers will benefit from the structure and coherence that these features lend to material that is often challenging. With Greenhaven's Literary Movements and Genres in hand, readers will be better able to comprehend and appreciate the major literary works and their impact on society.

INTRODUCTION

The genre of children's literature took shape very slowly and without much initial fanfare. The only way to trace its growth is through a study of its milestones—the books and authors and institutions that paved the way for the flourishing children's book industry of today. Scholars usually cite 1865's *Alice's Adventures in Wonderland* by British author Lewis Carroll as the first book of literature for children. It is true that *Alice* opened children's eyes to a world of laughter and the imagination, and influenced every children's author who followed. But even before the story of a little girl who went down a rabbit hole, children were reading tales of adventure and fantasy in the form of adult books like *Robinson Crusoe* or folk- and fairy tales like those from the Grimm brothers or Hans Christian Andersen. Other than those two categories, however, most of the earliest books for children were so didactic as to be painfully boring and stiff. Written purely to educate young minds on virtue, morality, and the alphabet, they never tried to entertain or excite the imagination.

Two books from the mid-1700s, however, proved that the world would one day be ready for *Alice* and its successors. They were John Newbery's *Little Pretty Pocket-Book* and *The Renowned History of Little Goody Two Shoes* by Oliver Goldsmith. Both books were intended to entertain their young readers, and if children learned a moral lesson along the way, all the better. On the heels of *Alice* came landmark books like Mark Twain's stories of Tom Sawyer and Huck Finn, Louisa May Alcott's *Little Women*, the fairy tale collections of Andrew Lang, the magic realism of E. Nesbit, and *The Tale of Peter Rabbit* by Beatrix Potter. Children now had a taste of books about fantasy, adventure, family life, magic, and animals all written for their enjoyment, starring children just like themselves. The floodgates were opened and a torrent of other children's books would follow.

By the dawn of the twentieth century, it was clear that

children's literature was expanding as fast as the society it began to reflect. Immigrants were pouring into America to make a better life for their children, and for the first time in history, society was keenly focused on educating its young. Children's librarians were trained, and publishing companies established separate departments to focus on creating books that children would want to read. Awards for excellence in children's literature were created, assuring that quality would continue to be cultivated. As modern life grew in complexity, books for children were written to keep pace with all the changes. Scientific advances, world wars, economic depression or growth all led to new fields of children's books while the tried-and-true topics from the nineteenth century proved still viable. After all, without fantasy there would have been no *Chronicles of Narnia* or, later, *Harry Potter;* without animal stories there would be no *Winnie-the-Pooh* or *Charlotte's Web.* New printing processes allowed books to be printed more cheaply and new color technology allowed artwork to be reproduced at a much higher quality than in the past. Children's books became a commodity, available not only in bookstores and libraries, but in supermarkets and variety stores, too.

Today, at the dawn of the twenty-first century, anywhere between two thousand and five thousand new children's titles are published in America each year, with nearly two hundred awards to honor them. Because the age range encompassed by children's literature extends from practically newborn through the teen years, the variety of formats and topics is naturally extensive. Each year brings new trends and new changes to a child's world, while the classics of the genre have proved to possess a timeless quality that appeals to generation after generation of children. This anthology is composed of essays written by some of the most well known critics and authors in the field of children's literature, both past and present. It is the editor's hope that this study will assist the reader in understanding the breadth and diversity, triumphs and controversies, of this extraordinary genre.

A Historical Overview
of Children's Literature

Storytelling has been an oral tradition ever since humans learned to communicate. In villages all over the world the elders of the group passed down stories of ancient lore told to them by their own ancestors. Usually the first stories children heard were based on their society's religious and cultural beliefs. It was not considered necessary for children to learn to read and write until well into the nineteenth century; thus, tales of the Greek and Roman gods and goddesses, or lessons from the Old and New Testaments of the Bible were kept alive through oral storytelling. Each region of the world developed its own stories about the great and wondrous things that had happened there, creating their own permanent collection of folklore, fairy tales, and fables. As the stories circulated orally, they evolved and were adapted to better represent a particular place in a particular time.

Before the invention of movable type in the mid-1400s, books were meticulously written and copied by hand, usually by monks in medieval religious orders. These men did not bother transcribing books for children. The few handwritten books that did circulate for young people were intended purely as educational tools to teach the wealthy child. It was much too expensive to reproduce them for the masses.

With the birth of the printing press, the ancient stories were finally immortalized in print and could be widely distributed. William Caxton was England's first printer; though religious texts were among the earliest printed works, Caxton decided to print tales he knew the literate public would eagerly buy—Sir Thomas Malory's *Tales of King Arthur* and the simple but wise *Aesop's Fables.* Even though these books were primarily for adults, children loved them as well.

The first book written exclusively for children was a book on table manners printed around 1487 in France. Though the subject matter was dull, the text was written in rhyme, and the book became very popular, as children enjoyed the lyrical and rhythmic nature of the language. It wasn't until centuries later that children would find joy in both the content and the words.

MOTHER GOOSE VERSUS MORALITY

In the 1600s and 1700s, two types of reading material became available to children. The first included pious, often morbid and depressing morality tales, and the other focused on stories of faraway places and fantastic deeds. When traveling peddlers began selling small (only a few square inches), handmade booklets called chapbooks, children were drawn to them. Filled with stories of ancient legends, ballads, and folktales, the booklets were either sewn together or simply folded. Adults disdained the folk- and fairy tales in these chapbooks, but children scraped together their pennies and couldn't wait until the peddler made another stop in their town. In England, according to one commentator, "Tudor and Stuart society had disapproved of folk tales because of their humble origins, the Puritans [both in England and America] had accused them of being frivolous and amoral; to the Age of Reason they were simply irrational and uncouth."[1] Most adults saw no use in children's reading beyond learning moral lessons, that is, how to be more godly or how to behave properly.

Favorites among the deeply religious Puritans who came from England to America were books like *A Token for Children: An Exact Account of the Conversion, Holy and Exemplary Lives and Joyful Deaths of Several Young Children.* This book, published in the early 1670s by clergyman James Janeway, featured thirteen grim tales intended to instill the fear of hell in its young readers. Another staple of Puritan education was *The New England Primer: An Easy and Pleasant Guide to the Art of Reading.* First published around 1691, verses like, "In Adam's Fall, We Sinned All"; "Thy Life to Mend, This Book Attend"; and "An Idle Fool is Whipt at School" suggest the book was not very pleasant after all.

Fortunately, publishers began to recognize the popularity of fairy tales and folktales, and in 1729 the first English version of *The Tales of Mother Goose* was published. This spirited and lighthearted collection of eight tales, including such well-loved stories as Cinderella and Sleeping Beauty, was credited to French author Charles Perrault. New editions of

the book with additional tales have been published continu-
ally ever since, and the name "Mother Goose" still conjures
up images of fairy tales and magical worlds. Soon, a few
brave authors began writing books for children with fresh,
new approaches.

FICTION, POETRY, AND THE GRIMM BROTHERS

In 1744, English publisher John Newbery issued *A Little
Pretty Pocketbook*, commonly considered the first original
book written purely for children's entertainment. To draw
children in, Newbery cleverly used the character of Jack the
Giant-Killer, already familiar from chapbooks. The re-
sounding success of this project paved the way for the first
children's novel, *The Renowned History of Little Goody Two
Shoes*, in 1765. Attributed to author Oliver Goldsmith, the
book tells the story of a poor girl who, out of the goodness of
her heart, travels the countryside teaching other young children how to read.

Though such original stories were taking hold, fairy tales
were certainly not forgotten. In 1823, a pair of siblings presented a definitive collection of fairy and folktales, gathered
from around the world and told in their own inimitable
style. The English edition of Jacob and Wilhelm Grimm's
collection contained hundreds of centuries-old stories, and
serves as the source for nearly all of today's modern fairy
tales. The Grimm brothers' versions of such tales as "Little
Red Riding Hood" and "Hansel and Gretel" are not the
pretty, comforting, "Disneyfied" versions that charm children today, however. The stories were rather dark and often
the characters didn't live happily ever after—no woodsman
arrived to rescue Little Red from the wolf in the original version. The Grimm brothers' collection was followed in 1846
by Hans Christian Andersen's lighter (yet still not cheery)
fairy tale adaptations. Fairy tales in general were given more
credibility when English novelist Charles Dickens wrote an
article stating that they nurture "forbearance, courtesy, kind
treatment of animals, and the love of nature in children."[2]
Over a hundred years later, child psychologist Bruno Bettelheim would go further and say that

> Of the entire "children's literature"—with rare exceptions—
> nothing can be as enriching and satisfying to child and adult
> alike as the folk fairy tale. . . . More can be learned from them
> about the inner problems of human beings, and of the right

solutions to their predicaments in any society, than from any other type of story within a child's comprehension.[3]

Poetry written for children also advanced during the 1700s and 1800s. In 1715, Isaac Watts produced a collection of comforting verses and hymns called *Divine and Moral Songs for Children*. The next big splash was William Blake's famous 1789 book of poems, *Songs of Innocence*. Although considered the finest example of book design and illustration of the eighteenth century, it was not as beloved by children as a collection called *Original Poems for Infant Minds* by Ann and Jane Taylor. Following on Blake's heels, the book included simple rhymes like "Twinkle, Twinkle Little Star," and it made the two sisters famous. Soon after, yet another pair of siblings, Charles Lamb and his sister Mary, came onto the literary scene. Their 1806 child-friendly adaptation, *Tales from Shakespeare*, is still considered the benchmark for all other books of its kind. In 1822, American professor Clement Moore wrote a long poem called *A Visit from St. Nicholas*. Better known as *The Night Before Christmas*, its fast-moving, humorous style became a turning point in the development of children's poetry and fiction.

A Picture's Worth a Thousand Words

The first full-length picture book for children was published in 1657 by a Moravian bishop and educator, Johann Amos Comenius. The book, titled *Orbis Pictus* (*The Illustrated World*) was the first to attempt to match images with words to help children better absorb the material. In 1844 a German picture book by Heinrich Hoffmann made a name for itself. *Struwwelpeter* (*Slovenly Peter*) was beloved for its silliness, in both text and art. A few decades later, a trio of great illustrators—Randolph Caldecott, Kate Greenaway, and Walter Crane—revolutionized the picture book industry. Since the advent of printing, illustrators had etched their work with tools or pencils onto wooden blocks or copper plates. These drawings were usually tiny—about the size of a postage stamp—and only a great artist could make these drawings come alive. But these three artists had a keen eye for design, and for the first time could produce their work in colors. This process breathed life into the illustrations, which began to claim greater space on the page. Books like Greenaway's *Under the Window* and Caldecott's *Hey Diddle* and *Baby Bunting* demonstrated that pictures and text to-

Illustrations, such as this one by Randolph Caldecott, revolution-ized the children's book industry by using pictures to enhance storytelling.

gether told a story that neither could alone. The picture book format continued to thrive with Wanda Gag's 1928 *Millions of Cats*, and modern writer-illustrators like Maurice Sendak proved that an exemplary picture book can stand among the finest children's literature.

WELCOME TO WONDERLAND

In 1865, Oxford mathematics professor Charles Lutwidge Dodgson—writing under the pen name Lewis Carroll—gave the world *Alice's Adventures in Wonderland,* and ushered in what would become a golden era of children's classics. At the time children's books were still a bit prosaic—Nathaniel Hawthorne in America was adapting the Greek myths, and Charles Kingsley had just published *The Water Babies* in England. Illustrated with whimsical drawings by Sir John Tenniel, *Alice* is considered the first great English novel written for children. There are no moral lessons, just flights of the imagination and wonderful wordplay. Pulitzer Prize–winning author Alison Lurie points out, "Alice, except for her proper manners, is by no means a good little girl in mid-Victorian terms. She is not gentle, timid, and docile, but active, brave and impatient. She is highly critical of her surroundings and of the adults she meets."[4] Children finally got to read about a character like themselves, who was not perfect, and who dreamed of an escape from her boring surroundings. The huge success of the book and its sequel, *Through the Looking Glass*, took its shy, unassuming author by surprise. Carroll's friend and colleague George MacDonald answered British children's clamor for more flights of fantasy with *The Light Princess* (1867) and *At the Back of the North Wind* (1871). Soon, E. Nesbit's unique brand of magical novels—beginning with *Story of the Treasure Seekers* in 1899—proved that fantasy was here to stay. Years later, J.R.R. Tolkien and C.S. Lewis, inspired by Nesbit's work, grandly continued the tradition.

In America, authors were responding to children's love of "Americana" with tales of outdoor adventure. Samuel Clemens, writing as Mark Twain, published *The Adventures of Tom Sawyer* in 1876 and *The Adventures of Huckleberry Finn* in 1884, as a rebuttal to what he called "goody-goody boys' books."[5] His main characters lie, steal, swear, and cheat, but young readers gladly went along on Tom and Huck's adventures. The "family saga" was also gaining momentum in both countries, and Englishwoman Charlotte Yonge produced well over a hundred family-centered books during the second half of the nineteenth century. In America, the success of Louisa May Alcott's *Little Women* (1867) paved the way for Laura Ingalls Wilder's *Little House* series a few decades later.

Another theme beloved on both sides of the Atlantic was the animal story. A number of those written around the turn of the twentieth century are still going strong a hundred years later. Rudyard Kipling's *The Jungle Book* (1894) and *Just So Stories* (1902), Beatrix Potter's *The Tale of Peter Rabbit* (1901) and Kenneth Grahame's *The Wind in the Willows*

(1908), set the stage for A.A. Milne's *Winnie-the-Pooh* and E.B. White's *Charlotte's Web* in the same way that Lewis Carroll's nonsensical verse was a precursor to Dr. Seuss's own inspired brand of spirited silliness.

BOOKS FOR A NEW TEEN AGE

By the turn of the twentieth century, nearly half of the population in America was under twenty years old. Stricter child labor laws were enforced and the mandatory years of education increased. These factors contributed to an elongated period of childhood and adolescence. Children weren't forced or expected to grow up as fast as in the past, and this extension of childhood has gradually lengthened. This new "teenager" had more leisure time, a sense of adventure, and loved a good story. In the first half of the century Edward Stratemeyer almost single-handedly delivered thirteen hundred novels written exclusively for them. He saw that children had few reading options besides cheap (and cheesy) adult dime novels, and a few children's magazines, which while very well written, didn't satisfy the hunger for full-length stories. Stratemeyer changed children's literature forever by creating 125 different book series including *Tom Swift, The Hardy Boys, The Bobbsey Twins, The Rover Boys,* and *Nancy Drew.* In 1926, the results of a poll conducted by the American Library Association showed that 98 percent of thirty-six thousand students rated Stratemeyer's series as their favorite books. This outcome appalled many librarians and teachers, who considered the books poorly written and not instructive in any way. It took many years before educators acknowledged that entertainment value, not to mention the fact that children were *voluntarily reading,* was good enough. The series book has remained a staple of children's literature ever since.

CHILDREN'S PUBLISHING BECOMES BIG BUSINESS

In 1919, National Children's Book Week was officially established in America, and Macmillan became the first publishing house to establish a children's department. According to one observer, the appointment of Louise Seaman as founding editor "would often be cited in later years as the beginning of children's book publishing in this country."[6] By the 1930s, nearly every publishing house had a children's book division, and two publishers—Holiday House and William R.

Scott—were devoted exclusively to publishing children's books. In all, nearly seven hundred children's titles were being published each year.

In 1921, Frederic G. Melcher, longtime editor of the trade journal *Publisher's Weekly* and champion of children's books and their authors, proposed that the American Library Association (ALA) honor high-quality children's books with a special annual award. The ALA created the Newbery Medal, named after the groundbreaking nineteenth-century publisher John Newbery. The award is given each year to the author whose book is selected as the most distinguished contribution to American literature for children. It assures the author's place in literary history and immortalizes the winning book. Beginning in 1938, and in honor of famed illustrator Randolph Caldecott, the Caldecott Medal is awarded annually to the finest American picture book. Award winners must have something special—an innovative plot combined with a unique voice and style. Both awards raised the standards and the prestige of children's literature.

For the next few decades, America's constantly changing society was reflected in the books for its children. The world wars prompted fiction and nonfiction children's books about war, peace, bravery, and the importance of understanding different cultures. New advances in science led to tales of science fiction just as the invention of the airplane led to stories of aviation. The works of British writers continued to be just as popular in America as they were at home, and over the next fifty years, children would be able to choose from an amazing variety of literary material, at affordable prices.

PUBLISHING IN THE SECOND HALF OF THE TWENTIETH CENTURY

Low reading scores on nationwide tests conducted in the 1950s caused educators to call for improved basic literacy in primary schools. The response from publishers was a rush of beginning reader books. Nonfiction books for children written in simple language also started filling library shelves. The number of children's books published annually doubled by 1960. Five years later, the federal government passed the Elementary and Secondary Education Act, which earmarked $1 billion for school library books, textbooks, and other instructional materials. At the time, nearly half of the elementary schools in the country lacked a school library. Publishing companies scrambled to produce more books and schools hurried to buy them with the new funds.

The turbulent sixties and soul-searching seventies heralded perhaps the greatest changes in books for older children—the birth of realistic fiction that dealt with contemporary social and coming-of-age issues. S.E. Hinton's *The Outsiders* and Judy Blume's *Are You There God? It's Me, Margaret* examined two very different kinds of teen angst and flew off the shelves. Gender roles became more flexible as girls and women took on more responsibilities and had more freedom. The star of Louise Fitzhugh's *Harriet the Spy* was a role model for female independence. As for the younger set, as the preschool and day-care movements strengthened, publishers saw the need for simple, playful books for toddlers. Bookstores just for children's books grew in number, and as publishers increasingly issued inexpensive paperback titles, children could purchase the books for themselves. These independent stores were very successful until they became overshadowed by the chain stores and superstores of the late 1980s and 1990s, whose large inventories allow them to sell books at a discount.

By the end of the 1980s, bookstore sales of children's books reached $1 billion. The spirit of Edward Stratemeyer returned in the middle of the decade with an upsurge in light series fiction suggesting to some that books that are not award-winning literature can still be a good read. Ann M. Martin's *The Babysitter's Club* and Francine Pascal's *Sweet Valley High* brought preteen girls back to the bookstores.

By the 1990s, horror series like R.L. Stine's *Goosebumps* (which brought preteenage boys to the bookstores) and tie-ins of popular television shows began to fill the stacks. Girl detective *Nancy Drew* was reborn, spun off into two new series, and modernized. Series for middle graders and younger children have become a way to get reluctant younger readers into the habit of reading for pleasure.

CHILDREN'S LITERATURE TODAY

Today's fast-paced and information-laden society provides a new challenge to children's book writers and publishers. To compete with cable television, computer games, and the Internet, children's book publishing has evolved from a labor of love into a cutting-edge, competitive business. Fiction, romance, horror, and mystery series continue to be churned out at the turn of the twenty-first century, as do novelty books ("how-to" or young storybooks packaged with toys or games), biographies of young actors and musicians, and adaptations of popular, youth-oriented television shows and movies. The merchandising that goes hand-in-hand with modern-day book publishing keeps the books alive longer. Children's books are now being made into television shows, movies, books-on-tape, and home videos. Stuffed toys and games based on characters from beloved classics can be found in most book and toy stores.

Commercialism aside, librarians, educators, reviewers, and parents take the quest for quality children's literature seriously. Teachers have integrated children's literature into their curriculum in their crusade to improve reading skills. Banning books often serves only to make them more popular, and if the groundbreaking success of British author J.K. Rowling's *Harry Potter* books is any example, children are embracing reading in record numbers. When the venerable *New York Times Review of Books* chose to rank the *Harry Potter* titles on their adult best-seller list, it elevated the status of children's literature across the board. Soon Rowling's millions of young fans will flock to the movie based on *Harry Potter and the Sorcerer's Stone.* Chances are they'll walk out and say, "Yeah, it was good. But the book was better."

NOTES

1. *Economist,* "Children's Books: Girls and Boys Wedded to Their Childish Toys," November 26, 1983, p. 95.

2. *Economist,* "Children's Books," p. 96.

3. Bruno Bettelheim, *The Uses of Enchantment: The Meaning and Importance of Fairy Tales.* New York: Random House, 1975, p. 5.

4. Alison Lurie, *Don't Tell the Grown-ups: Subversive Children's Literature.* Boston: Little, Brown, 1990, p. 17.

5. Lurie, *Don't Tell the Grown-ups,* p. 4.

6. Leonard S. Marcus, "Mother Goose to Multiculturalism," *Publisher's Weekly,* July 1997, vol. 244, no. 31, p. 62.

CHAPTER 1

Defining the Genre

Children's
Literature

What Is Children's Literature?

Margaret R. Marshall

Margaret R. Marshall, a librarian and educator, presents a simple explanation of what determines the boundaries of children's literature. She discusses the elements that make the books specifically geared for children—such as format, content, reading level—in an effort to show that those elements are exactly what defines the genre.

Literature for children, whether it is fiction or non-fiction, is part of the larger world of literature and can be written, read, studied, analysed, taught and promoted in the same way as literature for adults, or any other age or subject group.

In the same way as for adult literature it can be broken down into categories by form, into for example hardback, paperback, tape, picture book, junior novel, teenager novel; into fiction which can be subdivided into historical, animal, adventure, science fiction, fairy, school stories, humorous, social, and many other broad themes for story. It can be divided into series, sequels or into national categories such as English, American, Indian, African, German, Australian, Scottish or Japanese children's literature, and it can be further subdivided into age groupings such as 0–5, 6–8, 9–12, 13–19 or by reading ability groupings.

These are all external labels applied to certain texts and/or illustrations, but what are the factors which have caused the interested adult to pick out from literature in general those books that speak particularly to the minds and interests of children and young people?

1. Is there a kind of writing specifically suitable for children? This raises educational constraints. The term 'suitable' often means different things in different countries. In many Western countries it may mean morally suitable in the sense that certain themes are considered to be taboo in order to protect children from those aspects of adult life thought to be corrupting, unpleasant, or sexual. 'Suitable' may also refer to the education relevance. Perhaps the book may be thought to cover a theme, or be written in a style, that children cannot understand until a certain stage of mental, physical or reading development has been reached.

But there are many countries where 'suitable' books for children are achieved by requiring them to reflect the political, social or religious outlook of the State. This often produces books that can be called didactic, meaning intended to teach or to be instructional. Didacticism is a word frequently found in writings about children's books in many countries, particularly in the early years of English children's literature. . . .

2. Is there a literature aimed at children and therefore, by implication, not for reading by adults? This is even more arguable and makes it necessary to distinguish between books written *for* children and books *read* by children, and between books written for adults and books read by adults. Experience shows that in most countries where children are literate there is no rule which says that children cannot or must not read books supposed to be for adults, or vice versa.

There are numerous examples in English literature of books which are read and enjoyed by adults and children alike, such as *Alice in Wonderland* and *Winnie the Pooh*, both of which offer greater depths to the adult reader than to a child reader. Similarly from English 'adult' literature so-called adult books like Tolkien's *Lord of the Rings* and L.P. Hartley's *The Go-Between* attract young readers also.

The myths and legends whether read from books or heard via the storyteller are enjoyed by adults and children in every country.

Some writers say that they write for themselves rather than for an age group of reader, but other writers do have a child or a range of children in mind when they are writing a book, and they try to tailor the concepts, events and the vocabulary for that readership. In both cases some of the resulting books cross the very blurred dividing line between a book for children and a book for adults. So the author's aim or lack of it does not necessarily create a children's book. Children and adults read across whatever boundaries are made by publishers, librarians, teachers or parents.

3. Is children's literature a lower level of writing, a second-best training ground for writers who will then progress to writing for adults? This suggests that children are less intelligent than adults instead of simply knowing less than adults. Many writers of books write both adults and children's books. Some start with adult fiction or non-fiction and later write a book for children, others start with a children's book and then write for the adult market. Many alternate between the two over the years. Investigation of this aspect amongst established writers, past and contemporary in the English speaking world, would reveal that the great majority of authors of children's books also write adult books.

Many writers and illustrators say that children's literature requires much more research, attention to detail and careful writing for the text and art work, through there are of course many examples of second rate writing and illustration. In most countries children's books can be found in which it is obvious that little is expected of children and little is offered them.

Simplicity does not mean second rate. There are many simple books for young children and older, less able children which are very well thought through by the author, illustrator, designer and publisher. Equally there are many lengthy prose works which turn out to be examples of books in which the authors have not given sufficient thought to plot, style, characterization and vocabulary. So the length of the book and the density of the writing must not be equated with quality.

4. Is one of the distinguishing factors that the characters in the books are children? Some of the best known characters in literature confound this. Cinderella and Sleeping Beauty were past puberty; Big Claus and Little Claus and Ali Baba were adult baddies; Robin Hood, King Arthur, Pandora and Persephone were all adults; in fantasy fiction C.S. Lewis's Aslan, Tolkien's Hobbit, Grahame's Badger, Ratty and Mole are all adults in symbolized form, as are Anansi and Brer Rabbit. Most of Leon Garfield's characters are adult, so are Rosemary Sutcliff's. Mrs. Pepperpot, Mary Poppins, Raymond Briggs' Father Christmas and Fungus the Bogeyman are adults, as are Beatrix Potters's Mrs. Tiggywinkle and the people who live in Charles Keeping's *Railway Passage*. Most of the characters in the world's myths and legends were adults.

But there are many books which do have child characters and the good books relate the plot to the child's experience. In some cases it is an adult's view of a child's experience and, sometimes, an adult's view of what he thinks a child's experience ought to be. Child characters as such, are not necessarily a distinctive factor unless shown in relationship to the adult world or adult behaviour patterns, neither is child experience in terms of the so-called 'realistic' description of social setting or patterns of behaviour. This can be limiting to both writer and reader whereas the child's experience of *emotion* tends to be the same as an adult's. It may be much more intense because the child has not yet learned to control the emotions, and the emotion may pass more quickly because new experiences are crowding into a child's life at a fast rate. But books built upon the emotional aspects of the theme can cross national frontiers better than those based on a fixed time or place.

The experience of emotion and the description of social and emotional realism seem to come together most obviously in the genre of fiction known as the teenage novel. . . . Although the presence of a child character may not make the book a children's book the author's characterization of the child's emotions is a crucial factor.

5. What about language as a characteristic of children's literature? There is a common belief that for children, language, vocabulary and sentence structure involve writing 'down' by choosing simple words and shortening sentences to aid understanding. In picture books for the young child and for the retarded reader of any age this may be necessary. For these there are usually illustrations to give clues to the words in the text. But the writers who make concessions to vocabulary or structure unrelated to the theme of the book (unless it is for a 'special' readership), are likely to produce superficial and undemanding books. Short, simple words and sentences can be rich, as in the first page of Ted Hughes' *Iron Man.*

> The Iron Man came to the top of the cliff. How far had he walked? Nobody knows. Where had he come from? Nobody knows. How was he made? Nobody knows.

Short, simple sentences are effective in many of the myths, legends, and folklore tales, as in the story of *How Saynday Got the Sun*, from *North American Legends* edited by Virginia Haviland.

Then Saynday got busy because he'd finished his thinking. He
could begin to do things now.

'How far can you run?' he said to Fox.

'A long long way,' said Fox.

'How far can you run?' he said to Deer.

'A short long way,' said Deer.

'How far can you run?' he said to Magpie.

'A long short way,' said Magpie.

'I can't run very far myself,' said Saynday, 'So I guess I'll have
to take it last.'

Then he lined them all out and told them what to do.

In both cases the simplicity is rich and is helped by the repe-
tition of words which gives the story rhythm and a narrative
quality. Simplicity in these examples is part of the quality of
writing and is effective in the context. However in other
books large words and sentences may be needed to convey
mood, scene or conversation. Unusual words may create hu-
mour, impart information or indicate meaning in the context.

   6. *Perhaps the subject content is a means of categorizing a
book as a children's book?* But are there subjects which can
only be put into story form for children, or can only be offered to adults? The whole of human knowledge and experience in any period of time and any geographical place is
open to coverage in story form and in information book form.
The books that are suitable for children are those which look
at an aspect in a way with which a child, at his stage of
knowledge and development, can cope. Many of the great
themes in the story can give awareness, knowledge, and an
understanding of things which in real life might be over-
whelming. To many children what is real life for them is fantasy for others, depending upon their personal circumstances. So it is the *perspective* which creates a literature for
children, the angle from which the theme is viewed through
the characters, via the author. Whether the theme involves
world issues, morals, emotions, child or adult relationships,
peaceful or violent events, realistic or imaginary settings, animals, humans or objects, the angle of vision is what causes
a book to catch the interest of a child, the uniting of the mind
of the writer with the mind of the child. When the writer re-
captures the child-like vision, or as Rosemary Sutcliff de-

scribes herself, has a pocket of unlived childhood, or is in tune with contemporary childhood's needs and interests then the result is a book which enables the child to 'see' life and to acquire insight. This causes him not only to say 'That was a good book, have you any more?', but in many cases, to have the unspoken and subconscious satisfaction of adding to his stature mentally, emotionally and linguistically.

7. *What is children's literature?* It is the written word which collectively embraces all the features mentioned so far, subject matter, characters and settings, style of writing and use of vocabulary presented from an angle of vision which matches the child's perspective. 'Good' literature is that which also increases his perception. But this body of literature is made up of thousands of individual books, each the product of someone's brain, each different from the other, providing for differing languages, differing interests, differing needs and differing levels of reading ability.

However good a book is and however marketed, promoted and recommended, we cannot say that *every* child must read the book, or *every* child will enjoy the book, for a child will not read voluntarily unless he enjoys the experience or needs the information, any more than adults will, voluntarily, spend time on books which do not engage their minds or their hearts.

Children's Literature Sustains Its Own Genre

Clifton Fadiman

Essayist and reviewer Clifton Fadiman has taken on the task of explaining why books for children are not only important, necessary, and thriving, but why they deserve to form a "literature" able to stand on its own, with its own guidelines and goals. It took a long time for literary historians to even recognize children's literature as a separate genre, and once they did, it took even longer to dismiss the idea that children's books were inferior literature because they were written on a simpler level than regular books for adults.

If a children's literature is to exist as "an intelligible field of study," in [English historian] Arnold Toynbee's phrase, it must justify that existence on grounds beyond its contribution to mainstream literature. It must assert some qualified claim as a sovereign state, however small. Even if a cultural sirocco were instantaneously to dry up the mainstream, a children's literature would still have to show that it is identifiable as an entity.

On the surface the literature seems to need no defense. If it is but a by-product, what is the meaning of the avalanche of children's books that annually descends upon the bookstores? What shall we say of the thousands of children's book editors, authors, artists, anthologists, librarians, professors— even critics? Is there not a gigantic, nearly worldwide industry, working away to satisfy the child's demand for something to read—or at any rate the parents' demand for something to give the child to read? Can we not, like [English author] Samuel Johnson kicking the stone to refute Bishop Berkeley's theory of the nonexistence of matter, merely point to the solid reality and say, "I refute it thus!"?

No, we must do a little better than that, just as Johnson should have known that kicks and phrases, however forcible, do not really dispose of idealism in episcopal gaiters. Let us therefore first glance briefly at the case against a children's literature.

CHILDREN'S BOOKS AS AN INFERIOR GENRE

The man-in-the-street puts it in simple terms: children's literature cannot amount to much because "it's kid stuff." The assumption here is that by nature the child is "inferior" to or less than the adult. His literature must be correspondingly inferior or less. Give the kid his comic, while I read grown-up books. But does not this amiable condescension shelter a certain insecurity? As racism is the opium of the inferior mind, as sexual chauvinism is the opium of the defective male, so child-patronage may be the opium of the immature adult. This [essay] . . . not surprisingly, admits that in certain ways the child is patently inferior, but goes on to maintain that as an imaginative being—the being who does the reading—he is neither inferior nor superior to the adult. He must be viewed as the structural anthropologist views the "primitive"—with the same unsentimental respect, the same keen desire to penetrate his legitimate, complex symbol-system and idea-world.

There is, however, a more sophisticated case against a children's literature. Scholars have expressed it both negatively and positively.

Negatively the thing is done by omission. Literary historians leave out children's literature, as they might leave out the "literature" of pidgin-English. The English novelist Geoffrey Trease offers a key example. He refers to "Legouis and Cazamian's *History of English Literature,* in which no space is found, in 1378 pages, for any discussion of children's books and the only Thomas Hughes mentioned is not the immortal author of *Tom Brown's Schooldays,* but an obscure Elizabethan tragedian." Further examples are legion. Marc Slonim's authoritative *Modern Russian Literature from Chekhov to the Present* (1953) has no mention of Kornei Chukovsky as children's author. Hester R. Hoffman's *Reader's Adviser* (1964) finds space in its 1300 pages for a bibliography of Lithuanian literature, but not for Louisa May Alcott. C. Hugh Holman's *A Handbook to Literature* (1972) is alert to inform us about weighty literary matters from *abecedarius* to *zeugma*, but not about children's literature. That phenomenal compendium *Die Literaturen der Walt in ihrer mündlichen und schriftlichen Überlieferung*, edited by Wolfgang v. Einsiedel (1964), covers 130 assorted literatures, including the Malagasy, but from its 1400 pages you would never suspect that some writers have written for children. In Volume II of David Daiches' standard *A Critical History of English Literature* we find an otherwise excellent account of Kipling, but one from which we would never guess that he wrote masterpieces for children. While it is only fair to say that there do exist literary histories and reference manuals, notably those of recent years, that acknowledge children's books, the normal (and influential) stance of scholarship has been one of unconscious put-down by omission.

A few critics are more explicitly skeptical. In 1905 Benedetto Croce wrote: "The art of writing for children will never be a true art"; and again: "The splendid sun of pure art cannot be tolerated by the as yet feeble eye of the young." He argued also that the writer's ever-present consciousness of his child public inhibited his freedom and spontaneity.

In our time, too, there have been some thoughtful students to echo Croce's negative judgment. They claim that they cannot trace a sufficiently long tradition or identify an adequate number of masterworks. Robert Coles, for instance, who has himself done much to increase our understanding of the current juvenile literary scene, cannot find in the literature "style, sensibility, vision."

As long ago as 1896, the German educationist Heinrich Wolgast aroused a storm of controversy, echoes of which are still heard, merely by his statement that "creative children's literature must be a work of art." In 1969 the French scholar Isabelle Jan felt it necessary to begin her book with the question: "Does a children's literature exist?" Three years later, in a thoughtful article, "The Classics of French Children's Literature from 1860 to 1950," she gave a cautious answer to her question, confining the issue to her own country: "French children's literature . . . does not constitute a *literature* in the strict sense. Quite unlike English children's literature it has neither continuity nor tradition."

It is apparent that the esteem in which any vocation is held affects its development. If children's literature is not generally felt to be an identifiable art, important in its own right, potentially creative minds will not be drawn to it, and it will languish or become a mere article of commerce. . . .

CHILDREN'S LITERATURE HAS A TRADITION

Apologists must at once concede that the children themselves couldn't care less. For them, books are to be read, not analyzed; enjoyed, not defended. They are only mildly curious as to who writes them, except insofar as a Richard Scarry, a Joan Walsh Anglund or a Maurice Sendak operates, like Wheaties, as a brand name. They do, of course, vigorously favor one book over another, but hardly on the basis of any rationale of values. Nor do they, unlike adults, show much interest in being up-to-date in their reading. The annual juvenile best-seller lists are loaded with titles first published a score of years ago. Children are proof against literary fads, literary gossip, and especially literary critics. For them, books are no more literature than street play is physical exercise. The defense of their literary kingdom they cheerfully leave to their elders.

This elder rests that defense on the following grounds.

First comes the slippery concept we call tradition. A literature without a traceable history is hardly worthy of the name. If we relax our definition to the point of zero tension, children's literature may claim a foggy origin in St. Anselm's eleventh-century *Elucidarium,* possibly the first book of general information for young students. That would take our "tradition" back about 900 years. But common sense tells us that the good saint is no true source. He no more begat Lewis Carroll than the eleventh-century author of the *Ostromir Gospel* (often cited as the beginning of Russian literature) begat Dostoevsky.

Moving ahead a few hundred years we encounter an unidentifiable German who, between 1478 and 1483, issued *Der Seele Trost* ("The Soul's Consolation"), a religious tract explicitly addressed to children. Though valueless as literature, it may claim a little more legitimacy than the *Elucidarium.* One can view it as the *Urvater* [origin] of that long succession of moral tales that by this time should have turned children into paragons of virtue. If we reject *Der Seele Trost* we might accept as a point of origin Jörg Wickram's *Der jungen Knaben Spiegel* ("The Boy's Mirror"), perhaps the first "realistic" novel aimed at youth. Appearing in 1555, it would make children's literature date back over 400 years. And so we could proceed, making more and more plausible claims as we approach modern times, until we come to *A Little Book for Little Children*, by "T.W." The authority Percy Muir, dating it around 1712, considers it one of the first books designed for the entertainment of little ones. Push on a few years. In 1744 we meet John Newbery's publication *A Little Pretty Pocket-Book*, from which English children's literature is conventionally dated. But at once we recall that Perrault's fairy tales appeared almost half a century prior to this; and from the head of Perrault French children's literature may be said to spring.

Perhaps it is fair to say, then, that our field of inquiry, strictly defined, is nearly 300 years old; less strictly, perhaps 500 years old. How many mainstream literatures can claim an equally venerable tradition?

QUALITY WORKS FROM QUALITY WRITERS

Second comes the matter of masterpieces. Here we must admit that unfortunately one word must serve two somewhat different meanings. *Oedipus Rex* is a masterpiece. But so is *Mother Goose*. Both are true to human nature. Beyond that they have little in common. It will require further discussion to determine what makes a masterpiece in our field. At this point I assert dogmatically that in its 300-plus years of history the literature has produced first-order works of art in sufficient number to support our case. I can think of about fifty that merit discussion at length. Some are already classics in the simple sense that, enduring over the decades or centuries, they are still enjoyed by large numbers of children. Indeed, are they not more naturally "classical" than many mainstream classics? It takes the whole educational machinery of the French Republic to sell its boys and girls on Corneille. But Perrault, Jules Verne, even Madame de Ségur seem to survive by their own vitality. To the nuclear core of individual high-quality works we should add the total *oeuvre* of another fifty outstanding writers whose product as a whole is impressive but of whom we cannot so confidently assert that any single book stands out. Some of these are: Lucy Boston, Colette Vivier, E. Nesbit, Arthur Ransome, William Mayne, Eleanor Farjeon, René Guillot, Paul Berna, Tove Jansson, Gianni Rodari, Joan Aiken, Hans Baumann, José Maria Sanchez-Silva, Rosemary Sutcliff, David McCord, William

Pène Du Bois, James Krüss, John Masefield, I.B. Singer, E.L. Konigsburg, Ruth Krauss, Kornei Chukovsky, Henri Bosco, Madame de Ségur, Ivan Southall.

In our view any literature worthy of the name also gains in health and variety through the nourishment supplied by writers of the second or third class, even by writers commonly scorned as purveyors of mass reading. Children's literature is rich in writers of ephemeral appeal and even richer in manufacturers of unabashed trade goods. But in a way this circumstance strengthens rather than weakens our case. The ladder theory of reading must not be swallowed whole. Yet it is true that children often normally work up from Enid Blyton or *Nancy Drew* to more challenging literature, whereas a *kitsch*-happy adult tends to stay *kitsch*-happy.

SOME IDEAS ARE BEST TRANSMITTED THROUGH CHILDREN'S BOOKS

Third, our case rests also on the fact that, like science fiction, children's literature is a medium nicely adapted to the development of certain genres and themes to which mainstream media are less well suited. In "On Three Ways of Writing for Children" C.S. Lewis remarks that the only method he himself can use "consists in writing a children's story because a children's story is the best art form for something you have to say: just as a composer might write a Dead March not because there was a public funeral in view but because certain musical ideas that had occurred to him went best into that form." In the same essay, referring to E. Nesbit's Bastable trilogy, he speaks of the entire work as "a character study of Oswald, an unconsciously satiric self-portrait, which every intelligent child can fully appreciate"; and goes on to remark that "no child would sit down to read a character study *in any other form*" (italics supplied).

The major genre (perhaps nonsense verse is just as major) whose development is largely the work of children's literature is fantasy. Adult fantasies of a high order of course exist. But the form seems, for reasons we shall later examine, peculiarly suited to children; and children seem peculiarly suited to the form. Consequently we can trace a long line of fantasies, growing constantly in expressiveness and intricacy. MacDonald, Carroll, Collodi, Baum, de la Mare, Barrie, Lagerlöf, Grahame, Aymé, Annie Schmidt, C.S. Lewis, Tolkien, Saint-Exupéry, Rodari, Juster, Hoban—these are a few of the many writers who have found children's fantasy well fitted to statements about human life that are conveyable in no other way. While a fairy tale for grownups sounds spurious, the fairy tale for children still has successful practitioners.

There are certain experiences we have all had which, though also handleable in adult fiction, seem to take on a higher authenticity in juvenile fiction. For example, moving. For the child, moving from one neighborhood to another may be as emotionally involving as a passionate love affair is to the adult. For the adult a new neighborhood is a problem in practical adjustment; for the child, who must find a fresh peer-group to sustain him, it can be another planet.

RESONANT SYMBOLS

But it is not only minor themes, such as moving, or major genres, such as fantasy, to which children's literature throws open its portals. It also offers a natural home for certain symbols frequently held to be part of our unconscious, and universally present in myth.

Take the Cave. The Cave has an eerie, backward-transporting effect on us all, a sacral mix of awe, terror, and fascination. Whether this is linked to racial recollection, to persistent memory of the womb, or to some still undiscovered kink in the psyche, we may never know. But we have all observed that the unnameable Cave-feeling is peculiarly marked in the child. With no real cave available, we will, out of a chair or a huddle of blankets, construct a reasonable facsimile. It is therefore not surprising to find in his literature a body of work ringing the changes on this "archetypal" symbol. It is no accident that Alice starts her dream life by falling through a hole in the ground; or that the most recallable episode in *Tom Sawyer* occurs in a cave. Richard Church's *Five Boys in a Cave*—an excellent suspense story—stands as the perfect type of a whole school of speleological literature, mainly for boys. France, a great land for caves, offers many examples. We can go back as far as 1864 to Jules Verne's *A Journey to the Center of the Earth,* which is really about a vast cavern. Indeed his masterpiece, *20,000 Leagues Under the Sea* (1870), may be read as a vision of a watery cave. Exactly a century later Norbert Casteret's *Dans la nuit des cavernes,* extremely popular with the young, continued to exploit the theme. One of the works of nonfiction that retains its appeal is Hans Baumann's *The Caves of the Great Hunters* (German publication 1961). This deals with caves and other prehistoric sites actually discovered by boys and girls—and in one case by a dog, an animal that long ago became a first-class citizen of the republic of childhood. There is, too, Sonnleitner's vast, curious *Die Höhlenkinder,* whose first part was published as long ago as 1918 and which, despite its almost archaic tone, refuses to die. Over 300,000 copies have been sold in the German edition, and only a few years ago it was translated into English.

The Cave is but one of a group of themes, freighted with symbolic content, that find powerful development in children's literature. Related to its magical appeal is the child's affinity for the nonartificial, or for places man has abandoned to nature. A vast apparatus is needed to condition the human being to the fabricated, technological surround to which he now seems fated. But, until so conditioned, the child normally relates himself to a nontechnological world, or its nearest approximation. "The literature of childhood," remark the Opies [renowned British husband and wife folklorists], "abounds with evidence that the peaks of a child's experience are not visits to a cinema, or even family outings to the sea, but occasions when he escapes into places that are disused and overgrown and silent." Dozens of children's writers know and feel this, foremost among them William Mayne. Only Samuel Beckett has made grownup literature out of a dump. But in children's stories it is a familiar background, and it must be in part because such abandoned environments represent a grotesque triumph over the forces of "progress," forces the child must be *taught* to respect.

In short, any public defender of a children's literature will rest part of his case on the medium's high esthetic capacity to embody certain specific themes and symbolic structures, often more imaginatively than does the mainstream.

But the advocate must go beyond this. A body of writing ambitious to be called a literature may point to a tradition. It may claim to include a fair number of masterworks. It may make certain statements with marked effectiveness. But it must also demonstrate that it has both scope and the power to broaden that scope. A specialized, nonadaptive literature risks the fate of the dinosaur.

First, as to scope. Obviously children's literature cannot boast the range, amplitude, inclusiveness of general literature. General literature records human experience; and human experience, though not absolutely, is by and large a function of the flow of time. The child's book, though not limited to the reflection of his actual experience, is limited by what he can understand, however dimly; and understanding tends to enlarge with experience.

But we must not be too quick to pass from the dimensions of length and breadth to that of depth, and say that children's books can never be as "deep." The child's world is smaller than the grownup's; but are we so sure that it is shallower? Measured by whose plumbline? Is it not safer to say that, until the child begins to merge into the adolescent, his mental world, though of course in many respects akin to that of his elders, in many others obeys its own private laws of motion? And if this is so, it might be juster to use one plumbline to measure the depth of his literature, and a somewhat different one for that of his elders. No one will deny the depth of Dostoyevsky's Grand Inquisitor episode. But who is to say that, to a sensitive child reader, William Mayne's *A Game of Dark* does not convey an equally profound intimation of the forces of evil? Here are six lines of a "song" called *Firefly*, by Elizabeth Madox Roberts. A seven-year-old child, who happened to be a genius, might have written it; and any seven-year-old child can read it with pleasure.

> A little light is going by,
> Is going up to see the sky,
> A little light with wings.

> I never could have thought of it,
> To have a little bug all lit
> And made to go on wings.

The child who feels all that these six lines convey (especially the fourth) is caught up in profound reflection on the very nature of creation. The esthetic experience is for the child no less rich than would be for the adult a reading of Eliot's *Four Quartets*. The scale differs, the "thickness" does not.

To return to the matter of scope: it is clear that traditionally the child's literature has been closed (nowadays there are narrow apertures) to certain broad areas of human experience: mature sexual relationships, economic warfare in its broadest aspects, and in general the whole problematic psychic universe that turns on the axletree of religion and philosophical speculation. That vast library generated by [Spanish existentialist Miguel de] Unamuno's "tragic sense of life" is one that—though there are certain exceptions—is not micro-reflected in the child's books. Though again one must qualify, his is a literature of hope, of solutions, of open ends. To say that is to acknowledge the limits of its scope.

But if we turn to form rather than content, the judgment becomes a little less clear-cut. Children's literature contains no epic poems, not only because it developed long after the age of the epic but because its audience is ill-suited to the epic length. As for its lyric poetry, it includes several forms—nonsense verse, nursery rhymes, street rhymes, lullabies—in which the adult lyric tradition is comparatively defective. But in general its verse forms are simple and restricted as against the variety and complexity of mainstream verse. The literature contains little drama, whether in prose or verse, worth serious attention. It has so far evolved nothing closely resembling the traditional essay, although in an acute comment Jean Karl points to its remarkable powers of mutation: "Who would have dreamed that the familiar essay, no longer popular with adults, would suddenly be found in children's books, presenting all sorts of abstract ideas in picture-book form?" The reference here is to what is often called "concept books." A first-rate example is James Krüss's *3 × 3*, pictures by Eva Johanna Rubin, which is essentially a graphic expository essay on the abstract idea of three-ness.

But almost all the other major genres, whether of fact or fiction, are represented. Some, like the ABC book and the picture book, are virtually (as would naturally be the case) unique to the literature. So, in the same way, are children's books written by children themselves: Daisy Ashford's *The Young Visiters* (1919), surely one of the dozen funniest books in English, or *The Far-Distant Oxus* by Katharine Hull and Pamela Whitlock, written when the authors were fourteen and fifteen respectively. Children's fiction can be so experimental as to be reactionary: Gillian Avery has written Victorian novels that are not parodies or pastiches, but interesting in themselves.

CHILDREN'S LITERATURE EMBRACES MOST LITERARY FORMS

Most fictional forms one can think of are represented on the children's shelves. Some, such as the fairy tale, the fantasy, the fable, the animal story and the adventure yarn, can be found there in rich and highly developed profusion. The historical novel, especially in England, flourishes to a degree that makes it possible to hail Rosemary Sutcliff *tout court* as one of the best historical novelists using the language. Even the minor genre of the detective story is represented, long before Poe, in Mrs. Barbauld's *The Trial* (mid-1790s).

There are dozens of sub-genres and sub-sub-genres that are by nature given special prominence in children's literature: certain kinds of jokes and riddles; stories of toys and dolls, stuffed animals, animated objects; "bad boy" and "bad girl" stories; "career novels"; a whole school of chimney-sweep stories; children's puppet plays; "waif" novels; the school story; the vacation novel; and many others. We do not dispose of the matter when we say that these forms are simply a response to the child's natural interests, any more than we dispose of Proust when we say that his work is a response to the adult's interest in depth psychology. In both cases literature is enriched by the evolution of fresh vehicles for the imagination.

While no absolutely first-rate history or biography has been written for children, I would claim that the field has produced at least one masterly autobiography, on its own level as worthy of study as the *Confessions* of Rousseau or St. Augustine: Laura Ingalls Wilder's *Little House* series.

It is fair to say, then, that the scope of our literature, though it has its lacunae, is astonishingly broad. But it is not only broad. It has the capacity to broaden further, to invent or assimilate new forms, themes and attitudes, to devise original techniques of exposition and narration. The texts of Maurice Sendak are as "new" in their way as Joyce's *Ulysses* once was. So is the picture book itself, really a product of modern times, with its power to tell a story simultaneously in two mediums: Else Holmelund Minarik's *Little Bear* series illustrates this well. The all-picture book has evolved even more ingenious modulations: Mitsumasa Anno's dreamlike series of gravity-defying, non-Euclidean *Jeux de Construction* is only one startling example. The trick three-dimensional book (pop-ups, for example), though hardly part of literature, is nonetheless ingenious, satisfying, and a specific response to the child's desire to manipulate, change, construct.

Finally, as we shall see, contemporary children's literature has in the last decade or so found it possible to handle, even if not always successfully, a whole constellation of themes it was formerly denied: everything from drug addiction to homosexuality. . . .

THE INSTITUTION ALREADY EXISTS

To complete our case for a children's literature I offer two last considerations, one turning on the matter of scholarship, the other on the matter of institutions. Both may be debater's points. I concede that they are less persuasive than the arguments already adduced. All they do is point to the probability of the literature's existence. In themselves they do not constitute firm evidence of its high quality or organic integrity.

A literature is the sum of its *original* communications, especially its better ones, more especially its best. It is hard for us to meditate upon a literature as an intelligible field of study until the non-original communicator, the theorist and historian, have worked upon it. Had Aristotle never lived, classical Greek literature would still rank supreme. Nonetheless the *Art of Poetry* helps us to perceive its topography and distinguish its boundaries. We are trying at the moment to establish such topography and boundaries for a children's literature. Now the specific identity of any art becomes more firmly established as it develops self-consciousness. Of that self-consciousness critics, scholars, and historians are the expression.

It would seem that you cannot produce a theory without something to theorize about, nor a history without something to chronicle. Or is this always true? A. Merget's *Geschichte der deutschen Jugendliteratur* ("History of German Juvenile Literature") appeared in 1867, before the existence of any literature worthy of the name. But this striking example of German thoroughness does not completely undermine the feeling we have, when we see a signpost, that it is probably pointing to some place that is actually there.

Ten years ago, when I started this project, I thought all I had to do was read a few thousand original communications called children's books, think about them, and arrange my thoughts on paper. I knew, of course, that there were several standard histories which should probably be read too. But soon I became aware that there were almost (well, not quite) as many books *about* children's literature as there were books *of* children's literature, and that anyone who wished to do more than merely rationalize a set of impressions would have to become familiar with a learned corpus of astonishing proportions.

In one of his few transparent lines of verse Mallarmé complains

La chair est triste, hélas! et j'ai lu tous les livres.
[The flesh is sad, alas, and all the books are read.]

I can subscribe to neither half of the hexameter. Even after ten years' sampling of the scholarly literature, my flesh remains moderately cheerful; and it is a dead certainty that I have not read all the books. No one could. Few disciplines of such modest dimensions have evoked so much commentary as that associated with children's books and reading. The children themselves would be dumbfounded, perhaps exploding into hilarious laughter, could they realize what alps of research and theory have been reared since Perrault, his eye on both young and old, first set down the tale of Little Red Riding-Hood.

I intend no mockery. The body of criticism and history is not only formidable; it is valuable. It points up to the importance of what at first might seem a minor field of investigation. Though some of it, inevitably, is but dusty poking into the deservedly dead, and much of it duplicative, yet as a whole it reflects a solid tradition, of acute importance in the shaping of the minds and hearts of children.

There are few "developed" countries that have not produced a scholarly literature. It is vast in the cases of the United States, Britain, most of Europe, including Soviet Russia, and Japan. While I have not yet met with such material from Liberia, I have pored over Paul Noesen's *Geschichte der Luxemburger Jugendliteratur,* keeping in mind that the population of Luxembourg, counting every child, is 336,500.

True, the burden of our case rests on the original communications rather than on the commentaries. But it is only fair to set against such doubting Thomases as Coles and Croce the counterweight of a host of creative writers and thoughtful scholars for whom a children's literature is as much *there* as his mountain was for [British mountain climber George Leigh] Malory. Among the creators of that literature who have defended its integrity are James Krüss, Eleanor Cameron, Maurice Sendak, I.B. Singer, J.R.R. Tolkien, C.S. Lewis, Kornei Chukovsky. Among the scholars who have analysed its properties, staked out its limits, and celebrated its charms are the Frenchman Paul Hazard, the Italian Enzo Petrini, the Swiss Hans Cornioley, the Englishman Brian Alderson, the Canadian Sheila Egoff, the Swede Eva von Zweigbergk, the Iberian Carmen Bravo-Villasante, the Netherlander J. Riemans-Reurslag, the Luxembourger Paul von Noesen, the Argentinian Dora Pastoriza de Etchebarna, the Mexican Blanca Lydia Trajo, the New Zealander Dorothy White, the Israeli Uriel Ofek, the Norwegian Jo Tenfjord . . . the catalogue, though not endless, is impressive.

The mere existence of institutions is, of course, no argument for the values they incorporate: the Mafia, one supposes, is as intricate and efficient an institution as one could well desire. Yet the complex world-network of children's libraries, book and record clubs, research centers, publishers, scholarly magazines, academies, book councils, "book weeks," prizes and awards, summer schools, writers' associations, radio and television programs (but switch on a red light here), illustration exhibits, book fairs—all this, while alloyed with commercialism, bureaucratization, cliqueishness, and a certain inappropriate solemnity, nevertheless demonstrates the existence of a large and lively world of children's literature.

On Three Ways of Writing for Children

C.S. Lewis

C.S. Lewis, the famed British professor, theologian, and writer of the Narnia series, presents his views on what makes a children's book a success. Lewis believes that a story should feed the imagination and be told in the format that best fits the message of the story, without talking down to the child. The child reader will then be able to take what he has learned back into the real world, where everything, in Lewis's view, will be tinged with the world of the fantastic.

I think there are three ways in which those who write for children may approach their work: two good ways and one that is generally a bad way.

I came to know of the bad way quite recently and from two unconscious witnesses. One was a lady who sent me the [manuscript] of a story she had written in which a fairy placed at a child's disposal a wonderful gadget. I say 'gadget' because it was not a magic ring or hat or cloak or any such traditional matter. It was a machine, a thing of taps and handles and buttons you could press. You could press one and get an ice cream, another and get a live puppy, and so forth. I had to tell the author honestly that I didn't much care for that sort of thing. She replied, 'No more do I, it bores me to distraction. But it is what the modern child wants.' My other bit of evidence was this. In my own first story I had described at length what I thought was a rather fine high tea given by a hospitable faun to the little girl who was my heroine. A man who has children of his own said, 'Ah, I see how you got to that. If you want to please grownup readers you give them sex, so you thought to yourself, "that won't do for children, what shall I give them instead? I know! The little blighters like plenty of good eating!"' In reality, however, I myself like eating and drinking. I put in what I would have liked to read when I was a child and what I still like reading now that I am in my fifties.

GIVING CHILDREN WHAT THEY WANT

The lady in my first example, and the married man in my second, both conceived writing for children as a special department of 'giving the public what it wants.' Children are, of course, a special public, and you find out what they want and give them that, however little you like it yourself.

The next way may seem at first to be very much the same, but I think the resemblance is superficial. This is the way of Lewis Carroll, Kenneth Grahame, and Tolkien. The printed story grows out of a story told to a particular child with the living voice and perhaps *ex tempore*. It resembles the first way because you are certainly trying to give that child what it wants. But then you are dealing with a concrete person, this child who, of course, differs from all other children. There is no question of 'children' conceived as a strange species whose habits you have 'made up' like an anthropologist or a commercial traveller. Nor, I suspect, would it be possible, thus face to face, to regale the child with things calculated to please it but regarded by yourself with indifference or contempt. The child, I am certain, would see through that. In any personal relation the two participants modify each other. You would become slightly different because you were talking to a child and the child would become slightly different because it was being talked to by an adult. A community, a composite personality, is created and out of that the story grows.

THE BEST WAY TO SAY SOMETHING

The third way, which is the only one I could ever use myself, consists in writing a children's story because a children's story is the best art-form for something you have to say: just as a composer might write a Dead March not because there was a public funeral in view but because certain musical ideas that had occurred to him went best into that form. This method could apply to other kinds of children's literature besides stories. I have been told that Arthur Mee never met a child and never wished to: it was, from his point of view, a bit of luck that boys liked reading what he liked writing. This anecdote may be untrue in fact but it illustrates my meaning.

Within the species 'children's story' the sub-species which happened to suit me is the fantasy or (in a loose sense of that word) the fairy tale. There are, of course, other sub-species. E. Nesbit's trilogy about the Bastable family is a very good specimen of another kind. It is a 'children's story' in the sense that children can and do read it, but it is also the only form in which E. Nesbit could have given us so much of the humours of childhood. It is true that the Bastable children appear, successfully treated from the adult point of view, in one of her grownup novels, but they appear only for a moment. I do not think she would have kept it up. Sentimentality is so apt to creep in if we write at length about children as seen by their elders. And the reality of childhood, as we all experienced it, creeps out. For we all remember that our childhood, as lived, was immeasurably different from what our elders saw. Hence Sir Michael Sadler, when I asked his opinion about a certain new experimental school, replied, 'I never give an opinion on any of those experiments till the children have grown up and can tell *us what really happened.*' Thus the Bastable trilogy, however improbable many of its episodes may be, provides even adults, in one sense, with more realistic reading about children than they could find in most books addressed to adults. But also, conversely, it enables the children who read it to do something much more mature than they realize. For the whole book is a character study of Oswald, an unconsciously satiric self-portrait, which every intelligent child can fully appreciate: but no child would sit down to read a character study in any other form. There is another way in which children's stories mediate this psychological interest, but I will reserve that for later treatment.

In this short glance at the Bastable trilogy I think we have stumbled on a principle. Where the children's story is simply the right form for what the author has to say, then of course readers who want to hear that will read the story or reread it at any age. I never met *The Wind in the Willows* or the Bastable books till I was in my late twenties, and I do not think I have enjoyed them any the less on that account. I am almost inclined to set it up as a canon that a children's story which is enjoyed only by children is a bad children's story. The good ones last. A waltz which you can like only when you are waltzing is a bad waltz.

FAIRY TALES OUTLIVE CHILDHOOD

This canon seems to me most obviously true of that particular type of children's story which is dearest to my own taste, the fantasy or fairy tale. Now the modern critical world uses 'adult' as a term of approval. It is hostile to what it calls 'nostalgia' and contemptuous of what it calls 'Peter Pantheism.' Hence a man who admits that dwarfs and giants and talking beasts and witches are still dear to him in his fifty-third year is now less likely to be praised for his perennial youth than scorned and pitied for arrested development. If I spend some little time defending myself against these charges, this is not so much because it matters greatly whether I am scorned and pitied as because the defence is germane to my whole view of the fairy tale and even of literature in general. My defence consists of three propositions.

1. I reply with a *tu quoque* [you, too (are guilty)]. Critics who treat *adult* as a term of approval, instead of as a merely descriptive term, cannot be adult themselves. To be concerned about being grownup, to admire the grownup because it is grownup, to blush at the suspicion of being childish— these things are the marks of childhood and adolescence. And in childhood and adolescence they are, in moderation, healthy symptoms. Young things ought to want to grow. But to carry on into middle life or even into early manhood this concern about being adult is a mark of really arrested development. When I was ten, I read fairy tales in secret and would have been ashamed if I had been found doing so. Now that I am fifty I read them openly. When I became a man I put away childish things, including the fear of childishness and the desire to be very grownup.

2. The modern view seems to me to involve a false conception of growth. They accuse us of arrested development because we have not lost a taste we had in childhood. But surely arrested development consists not in refusing to lose old things but in failing to add new things? I now like hock, which I am sure I should not have liked as a child. But I still like lemon-squash. I call this growth or development because I have been enriched: where I formerly had only one pleasure, I now have two. But if I had to lose the taste for lemon-squash before I acquired the taste for hock, that would not be growth but simple change. I now enjoy Tolstoy and Jane Austen and Trollope as well as fairy tales and I call that growth; if I had had to lose the fairy tales in order to acquire the novelists, I

would not say that I had grown but only that I had changed. A tree grows because it adds rings; a train doesn't grow by leaving one station behind and puffing on to the next. In reality, the case is stronger and more complicated than this. I think my growth is just as apparent when I now read the fairy tales as when I read the novelists, for I now enjoy the fairy tales better than I did in childhood: being now able to put more in, of course I get more out. But I do not here stress that point. Even if it were merely a taste for grownup literature added to an unchanged taste for children's literature, addition would still be entitled to the name 'growth', and the process of merely dropping one parcel when you pick up another would not. It is, of course, true that the process of growing does, incidently and unfortunately, involve some more losses. But that is not the essence of growth, certainly not what makes growth admirable or desirable. If it were, if to drop parcels and to leave stations behind were the essence and virtue of growth, why should we stop at the adult? Why should not *senile* be equally a term of approval? Why are we not to be congratulated on losing our teeth and hair? Some critics seem to confuse growth with the cost of growth and also to wish to make that cost far higher than, in nature, it need be.

3. The whole association of fairy tale and fantasy with childhood is local and accidental. I hope everyone has read Tolkien's essay on fairy tales, which is perhaps the most important contribution to the subject that anyone has yet made. If so, you will know already that, in most places and times, the fairy tale has not been specially made for, nor exclusively enjoyed by, children. It has gravitated to the nursery when it became unfashionable in literary circles, just as unfashionable furniture gravitated to the nursery in Victorian houses. In fact, many children do not like this kind of book, just as many children do not like horsehair sofas; and many adults do like it, just as many adults like rocking-chairs. And those who do like it, whether young or old, probably like it for the same reason. And none of us can say with any certainty what that reason is. The two theories which are most often in my mind are those of Tolkien and of Jung.

THE APPEAL OF FANTASY

According to Tolkien the appeal of the fairy story lies in the fact that man there most fully exercises his function as a 'subcreator'; not, as they love to say now, making a 'comment upon life' but making, so far as possible, a subordinate world of his own. Since, in Tolkien's view, this is one of man's proper functions, delight naturally arises whenever it is successfully performed. For Jung, fairy tale liberates the Archetypes which dwell in the collective unconscious, and when we read a good fairy tale we are obeying the old precept 'Know thyself'. I would venture to add to this my own theory, not indeed of the Kind as a whole, but of one feature in it: I mean, the presence of beings other than human which yet behave, in varying degrees, humanly—the giants and dwarfs and talking beasts. I believe these to be at least (for they may have many other sources of power and beauty) an admirable hieroglyphic which conveys psychology, types of character, more briefly than novelistic presentation and to readers whom novelistic presentation could not yet reach. Consider Mr Badger in *The Wind in the Willows*—that extraordinary amalgam of high rank, coarse manners, gruffness,

---

HOW TO CAPTURE A CHILD'S ATTENTION

Aidan Warlow, co-author of The Cool Web: The Pattern of Children's Reading, *warns that children's authors must hook the child's attention in the beginning scene, or else risk the child losing patience and reading no further.*

The child . . . picks a book from the shelf, or unpacks it on Christmas morning, or has it dumped on his desk by a teacher. And then he asks the crucial question 'Will it be any good?' His answer will depend largely on the matching of his personal needs with the expectations that he forms of the book after a rapid examination of the title, format, illustrations, and typography, reinforced perhaps by the comments on the dust-jacket and the opening sentences of the story. Drawing on his previous experience of comparable books, he has to decide whether the anticipated satisfactions are likely to outweigh the effort required to read it.

If these expectations prove favourable, he starts his reading. The early part of the story is the difficulty. At first, perhaps only for a sentence, perhaps for several pages, the reader is in a confused position. He does not know the location, characters, or situation of the novel (though the pictures, blurb, and his previous expectations may have helped). Then it all gradually becomes clear. This ambivalent period before 'getting into the story' is critical in deciding whether to go on or put the book aside.

shyness, and goodness. The child who has once met Mr Badger has ever afterwards in its bones a knowledge of humanity and of English social history which it could not get in any other way.

Of course as all children's literature is not fantastic, so all fantastic books need not be children's books. It is still possible, even in an age so ferociously anti-romantic as our own, to write fantastic stories for adults—though you will usually need to have made a name in some more fashionable kind of literature before anyone will publish them. But there may be an author who at a particular moment finds not only fantasy but fantasy-for-children the exactly right form for what he wants to say. The distinction is a fine one. His fantasies for children and his fantasies for adults will have very much more in common with one another than either has with the ordinary novel or with what is sometimes called 'the novel of child life'. Indeed the same readers will probably read

---

Clearly the period of confusion is very brief in stories which conform to familiar and predictable conventions, for example the traditional fairy story or the fourteenth Enid Blyton book. And some novelists make sure that we have all the essential data as early as possible. E.B. White opens *Charlotte's Web* with the words: '"Where's Papa going with that axe?" said Fern to her mother as they were laying the table for breakfast', which, with maximum economy of words, tells us the heroine's name, her family relationships and what she is doing at a particular time in the morning as well as alerting us to the rather ominous idea of a father wandering around with an axe. Other novelists keep us waiting longer. In *The Owl Service*, for example, Alan Garner keeps the reader confused as to who the characters *are* for several pages and it is not until the second chapter that we really grasp who is whose brother and which is the father. Meanwhile the reader is distracted by essential information being withheld.

It is the real test of the maturity of the reader to see how long he can tolerate this ambivalent period of doubt. If the fantasy experience is not forthcoming quite soon he may lose faith in the novel. The inexperienced reader cannot defer his gratification for long. The expectation of pleasure has to outweigh present dissatisfaction.

Margaret Meek, Aidan Warlow, and Griselda Barton, *The Cool Web: The Pattern of Children's Reading.* London: Bodley Head, 1977, pp. 91–96.

both his fantastic 'juveniles' and his fantastic stories for adults. For I need not remind such an audience as this that the neat sorting-out of books into age-groups, so dear to publishers, has only a very sketchy relation with the habits of any real readers. Those of us who are blamed when old for reading childish books were blamed when children for reading books too old for us. No reader worth his salt trots along in obedience to a time-table. The distinction then is a fine one; and I am not quite sure what made me, in a particular year of my life, feel that not only a fairy tale, but a fairy tale addressed to children, was exactly what I must write—or burst. Partly, I think that this form permits, or compels, you to leave out things I wanted to leave out. It compels you to throw all the force of the book into what was done and said. It checks what a kind but discerning critic called 'the expository demon' in me. It also imposes certain very fruitful necessities about length.

If I have allowed the fantastic type of children's story to run away with this discussion, that is because it is the kind I know and love best, not because I wish to condemn any other. But the patrons of the other kinds very frequently want to condemn it. About once every hundred years some wiseacre gets up and tries to banish the fairy tale. Perhaps I had better say a few words in its defence, as reading for children.

A SPECIAL KIND OF LONGING

It is accused of giving a false impression of the world they live in. But I think no literature that children could read gives them less of a false impression. I think what profess to be realistic stories for children are far more likely to deceive them. I never expected the real world to be like the fairy tales. I think that I did expect school to be like the school stories. The fantasies did not deceive me: the school stories did. All stories in which children have adventures and successes which are possible, in the sense that they do not break the laws of nature, but almost infinitely improbable, are in more danger than the fairy tales of raising false expectations.

Almost the same answer serves for the popular charge of escapism, though here the question is not so simple. Do fairy tales teach children to retreat into a world of wish-fulfilment—'fantasy' in the technical psychological sense of the word—instead of facing the problems of the real world? Now it is here that the problem becomes subtle. Let us again lay the fairy tale side by side with the school story or any other story which is labelled a 'Boy's Book' or a 'Girl's Book,' as distinct from a 'Children's Book.' There is no doubt that both arouse, and imaginatively satisfy, wishes. We long to go through the looking-glass, to reach fairyland. We also long to be the immensely popular and successful schoolboy or schoolgirl, or the lucky boy or girl who discovers the spy's plot or rides the horse that none of the cowboys can manage. But the two longings are very different. The second, especially when directed on something so close as school life, is ravenous and deadly serious. Its fulfilment on the level of imagination is in very truth compensatory: we run to it from the disappointments and humiliations of the real world; it sends us back to the real world undivinely discontented. For it is all flattery to the ego. The pleasure consists in picturing oneself the object of admiration. The other longing, that for fairyland, is very different. In a sense a child does not long for fairyland as a boy longs to be the hero of the first eleven. Does anyone suppose that he really and prosaically longs for all the dangers and discomforts of a fairy tale?—really wants dragons in contemporary England? It is not so. It would be much truer to say that fairyland arouses a longing for he knows not what. It stirs and troubles him (to his lifelong enrichment) with the dim sense of something beyond his reach and, far from dulling or emptying the actual world, gives it a new dimension of depth. He does not despise real woods because he has read of enchanted woods: the reading makes all real woods a little enchanted. This is a special kind of longing. The boy reading the school story of the type I have in mind desires success and is unhappy (once the book is over) because he can't get it: the boy reading the fairy tale desires and is happy in the very fact of desiring. For his mind has not been concentrated on himself, as it often is in the more realistic story.

I do not mean that school stories for boys and girls ought not be written. I am only saying that they are far more liable to become 'fantasies' in the clinical sense than fantastic stories are. And this distinction holds for adult reading too. The dangerous fantasy is always superficially realistic. The real victim of wishful reverie does not batten on *The Odyssey, The Tempest,* or *The Worm Ouroboros*: he (or she) prefers stories about millionaires, irresistible beauties, posh hotels, palm beaches, and bedroom scenes—things that really might happen, that ought to happen, that would have happened if the reader had had a fair chance. For, as I say, there are two kinds of longing. The one is an *askesis,* a spiritual exercise, and the other is a disease.

CAN BOOKS FRIGHTEN CHILDREN?

A far more serious attack on the fairy tale as children's literature comes from those who do not wish children to be frightened. I suffered too much from night-fears myself in childhood to undervalue this objection. I would not wish to heat the fires of that private hell for any child. On the other hand, none of my fears came from fairy tales. Giant insects were my specialty, with ghosts a bad second. I suppose the ghosts came directly or indirectly from stories, though certainly not from fairy stories, but I don't think the insects did. I don't know anything my parents could have done or left undone which would have saved me from the pincers, mandibles, and eyes of those many-legged abominations. And that, as so many people have pointed out, is the difficulty. We do not know what will or will not frighten a child in this particular way. I say 'in this particular way' for we must here make a distinction. Those who say that children must not be frightened may mean two things. They may mean (1) that we must not do anything likely to give the child those haunting, disabling, pathological fears against which ordinary courage is helpless: in fact, *phobias.* His mind must, if possible, be kept clear of things he can't bear to think of. Or they may mean (2) that we must try to keep out of his mind the knowledge that he is born into a world of death, violence, wounds, adventure, heroism and cowardice, good and evil. If they mean the first I agree with them: but not if they mean the second. The second would indeed be to give children a false impression and feed them on escapism in the bad sense. There is something ludicrous in the idea of so educating a generation which is born to the Ogpu [Soviet secret police] and the atomic bomb. Since it is so likely that they will meet cruel enemies, let them at least have heard of brave knights and heroic courage. Otherwise you are making their destiny not brighter but darker. Nor do most of us find that violence and bloodshed, in a story, produce any haunting dread in the minds of children. As far as that goes, I side impenitently with the human race against the modern reformer. Let there be wicked kings and beheadings, battles and dungeons, giants and dragons, and let villains be soundly killed at the end of the book. Nothing will persuade me that this causes an ordinary child any kind or degree of fear beyond what it wants, and needs, to feel. For, of course, it wants to be a little frightened.

The other fears—the phobias—are a different matter. I do not believe one can control them by literary means. We seem to bring them into the world with us ready made. No doubt the particular image on which the child's terror is fixed can sometimes be traced to a book. But is that the source, or only the occasion, of the fear? If he had been spared that image, would not some other, quite unpredictable by you, have had the same effect? Chesterton has told us of a boy who was more afraid of the Albert Memorial than anything else in the world. I know a man whose great childhood terror was the India paper edition of the *Encyclopaedia Britannica*—for a reason I defy you to guess. And I think it possible that by confining your child to blameless stories of child life in which nothing at all alarming ever happens, you would fail to banish the terrors, and would succeed in banishing all that can ennoble them or make them endurable. For in the fairy tales, side by side with the terrible figures, we find the immemorial comforters and protectors, the radiant ones: and the terrible figures are not merely terrible, but sublime. It would be nice if no little boy in bed, hearing, or thinking he hears, a sound, were ever at all frightened. But if he is going to be frightened, I think it better that he should think of giants and dragons than merely of burglars. And I think St George, or any bright champion in armour, is a better comfort than the idea of the police.

I will even go further. If I could have escaped all my own night-fears at the price of never having known 'faerie', would I now be the gainer by that bargain? I am not speaking carelessly. The fears were very bad. But I think the price would have been too high.

But I have strayed far from my theme. This has been inevitable for, of the three methods, I know by experience only the third. I hope my title did not lead anyone to think that I was conceited enough to give you advice on how to write a story for children. There were two very good reasons for not doing that. One is that many people have written very much better stories than I, and I would rather learn about the art than set up to teach it. The other is that, in a certain sense, I have never exactly 'made' a story. With me the process is much more like bird-watching than like either talking or building. I see pictures. Some of these pictures have a common flavour, almost a common smell, which groups them together. Keep quiet and watch and they will begin joining themselves up. If you were very lucky (I have never been as lucky as all that), a whole set might join themselves so consistently that there you had a complete story without doing anything yourself. But more often (in my experience always) there are gaps. Then at last you have to do some deliberate inventing, have to contrive reasons why these characters should be in these various places doing these various things. I have no idea whether this is the usual way of writing stories, still less whether it is the best. It is the only one I know: images always come first.

TREATING ALL READERS WITH RESPECT

Before closing, I would like to return to what I said at the beginning. I rejected any approach which begins with the question 'What do modern children like?' I might be asked 'Do you equally reject the approach which begins with the question "What do modern children need?"—in other words, with the moral or didactic approach?' I think the answer is Yes. Not because I don't like stories to have a moral: certainly not because I think children dislike a moral. Rather because I feel sure that the question 'What do modern children need?' will not lead you to a good moral. If we ask that question we are assuming too superior an attitude. It would be better to ask 'What moral do I need?', for I think we can be sure that what does not concern us deeply will not deeply interest our readers, whatever their age. But it is better not to ask the question at all. Let the pictures tell you their own moral. For the moral inherent in them will rise from whatever spiritual roots you have succeeded in striking during the whole course of your life. But if they don't show you any moral, don't put one in. For the moral you put in is likely to be a platitude, or even a falsehood, skimmed from the surface of your consciousness. It is impertinent to offer the children that. For we have been told on high authority that in the moral sphere they are probably at least as wise as we. Anyone who *can* write a children's story without a moral, had better do so: that is, if he is going to write children's stories at all. The only moral that is of any value is that which arises inevitably from the whole cast of the author's mind.

Indeed everything in the story should arise from the whole cast of the author's mind. We must write for children out of those elements in our own imagination which we share with children: differing from our child readers not by any less, or less serious, interest in the things we handle, but by the fact that we have other interests which children would not share with us. The matter of our story should be a part of the habitual furniture of our minds. This, I fancy, has been so with all great writers for children, but it is not generally understood. A critic not long ago said in praise of a very serious fairy tale that the author's tongue 'never once got into his cheek'. But why on earth should it?—unless he had been eating a seed-cake. Nothing seems to me more fatal, for this art, than an idea that whatever we share with children is, in the privative sense, 'childish' and that whatever is childish is somehow comic. We must meet children as equals in that area of our nature where we are their equals. Our superiority consists partly in commanding other areas, and partly (which is more relevant) in the fact that we are better at telling stories than they are. The child as reader is neither to be patronized nor idolized: we talk to him as man to man. But the worst attitude of all would be the professional attitude which regards children in the lump as a sort of raw material which we have to handle. We must of course try to do them no harm: we may, under the Omnipotence, sometimes dare to hope that we may do them good. But only such good as involves treating them with respect. We must not imagine that we are Providence or Destiny. I will not say that a good story for children could never be written by someone in the Ministry of Education, for all things are possible. But I should lay very long odds against it.

Once in a hotel dining-room I said, rather too loudly, 'I loathe prunes.' 'So do I' came an unexpected six-year-old voice from another table. Sympathy was instantaneous. Neither of us thought it funny. We both knew that prunes are far too nasty to be funny. That is the proper meeting between man and child as independent personalities. Of the far higher and more difficult relations between child and parent or child and teacher, I say nothing. An author, as a mere author, is outside all that. He is not even an uncle. He is a freeman and an equal, like the postman, the butcher, and the dog next door.

CHAPTER 2

The Growth of Children's Literature

Children's Literature

The Early Years of Children's Literature

Roger Lancelyn Green

Roger Lancelyn Green, the famed British literary
scholar, mythologist, novelist and biographer, is
uniquely qualified to present the humble beginnings
of children's literature. Most of these titles have been
lost to history by this time, but Green affectionately
brings these books back to life. He takes the reader
through the earliest "morality-themed" books,
through the adventure stories, into fantasy, everyday-
life, sentimentality, magic, and finally arrives at fully
realized children's stories.

There were few books written before the middle of the nineteenth century which can be said to have more than an an-
tiquarian interest today. Several adult books like *Robinson
Crusoe, Gulliver's Travels,* and *Baron Munchausen* which
have become nursery property (usually now in abridged or
simplified versions) are beside the point, as are ballads, popular rhymes, and folktales. Beyond a few translations of foreign fairy tales (Perrault and Grimm) and of *The Arabian
Nights,* Lamb's *Tales from Shakespeare* (1807) is the only
book from before the middle of the century which is still
read, or which deserves any place among children's classics.
Apart from this, and from a few representative poems in an-
thologies, Marryat's *The Children of the New Forest* (1847)
and Ruskin's *The King of the Golden River* (1851—but written some years earlier) are the only islands still visible in
those early waters.

The only book which hovers on the border between actual and academic interest is Catherine Sinclair's *Holiday
House* (1839). From the historical point of view it is one of
the most important books in the history of children's literature, for it was written with the intention of changing the

Excerpted from Roger Lancelyn Green, "The Golden Age of Children's Books," in *Only
Connect: Readings of Children's Literature*, edited by Sheila Egoff, G.T. Stubbs, and L.F.
Ashley. Copyright © 1969 Oxford University Press, Canada. Reprinted with permission
from Richard Lancelyn Green, literary executor of Roger Lancelyn Green.

quality and kind of reading supplied for young people, and it was so successful that not only did it achieve its purpose but it remained in print and was read by children for precisely a hundred years.

At a time when 'informative' books (they are now called, significantly, 'non-fiction') are once again swamping the junior-book counters, it is worth looking at what Catherine Sinclair wrote (for parents) in her preface:

Books written for young persons are generally a mere dry record of facts, unenlivened by any appeal to the heart, or any excitement to the fancy . . . but nothing on the habits and ways of thinking natural and suitable to the taste of children. Therefore, while such works are delightful to the parents and teachers who select them, the younger community are fed with strong meat instead of milk, and the reading which might be a relaxation from study becomes a study in itself . . .

In these pages, the author has endeavoured to paint that species of noisy, frolicsome, mischievous children which is now almost extinct, wishing to preserve a sort of fabulous remembrance of days long past, when young people were like wild horses on the prairies, rather than like well-broken hacks on the road; and when, amid many faults and many eccentricities there was still some individuality of character and feeling allowed to remain.

Her battle was not won without a long struggle, and her children seem fairly tame now in the light of subsequent developments. The only part of the book which stands out as a notable achievement that is still fresh and entertaining is the 'Wonderful Story' about Giant Snap-'em-up (who was so tall that he 'was obliged to climb up a ladder to comb his own hair'), which is the earliest example of Nonsense literature and a direct precursor of Lewis Carroll and E. Nesbit.

ROMANCES, MYTHS, AND FAIRY TALES

It was some time before either the nonsense fairy tale or the story of true-to-life childhood achieved any worthy representations; but meanwhile a new development was started by Marryat and developed by Charlotte Yonge—the simple historical romance, usually with a child hero. In an age when the Waverley Novels [of Sir Walter Scott] were read avidly even by young children (Mrs Molesworth, born 1839, was reading them at the age of six when *Peveril of the Peak* proved too difficult, though she had found *Ivanhoe* and *The*

Talisman 'so much nicer and easier'), and when Scott's followers such as Bulwer Lytton and Harrison Ainsworth were not forbidden like the majority of adult novels, it was natural that, sooner or later, such books would be written with the young reader specially in view. An obvious development came also by way of the 'desert island' story, since *Robinson Crusoe* and *The Swiss Family Robinson* had been followed by the intensely pious *Masterman Ready*. R.M. Ballantyne avoided the didactic brilliantly in *The Coral Island* (1858), and followed it with excellent adventure stories in other fields which, like the meticulously historical thrillers of G.A. Henty, grew together towards the close of the century into the semi-adult movement of the 'storytellers' headed by Stevenson, Haggard, and Conan Doyle.

The really distinctive children's book grew more slowly and in less expected forms. Traditional fairy tales and stories from myth and legend found a period of great popularity about the time of the first translation of Hans Andersen (1846) and of Kingsley's *The Heroes* (1856), the Kearys' *Heroes of Asgard* (1857) and Dasent's *Tales from the Norse* (1859). But the original tale of fantasy developed slowly. Probably the earliest of any was F.E. Paget's *The Hope of the Katzekopfs* (1844), which showed real imagination and invention, but gave way to an undue weight of direct moral teaching which cripples its last two chapters hopelessly. It has not been reprinted since a shortened version renamed *The Self-willed Prince* came out about 1908.

Ruskin's *The King of the Golden River* (1851), a brilliant imitation of Grimm, made the grade, though an interesting experiment in the Border Ballad tradition of fairy tale, by Mrs Craik, *Alice Learmont* (1852), failed to hold its audience. But at Christmas 1854 (though dated 1855), Thackeray produced the first classic of fairy-tale nonsense and set the stage for all future stories of the 'Fairy Court' with *The Rose and the Ring*.

Although there is a basic moral in Thackeray's fantasy, the story, the characters, and the spirit of fun are all more important. With the paradox of all true originality, Thackeray owed several debts for the materials with which he built: the general fairy-tale background of writers like Madame d'Aulnoy and the pantomime tradition which was growing in the able works of Planché and H.J. Byron; perhaps *The Hope of the Katzekopfs*, certainly Fielding's heroic burlesque *Tom Thumb the Great* whose language is echoed in the royal blank verse and in the brilliant use of bathos ('He raised his hand to an anointed King, Hedzoff, and floored me with a warming pan!' 'Rebellion's dead—and now we'll go to breakfast').

The Rose and the Ring had very few direct followers, or few that survive. Tom Hood 'the Younger' wrote probably the best imitation, *Petsetilla's Posy* (1870), though it is too like its original to escape destructive criticism, and there were others of even less importance. It was not, in fact, until thirty-five years later that a major work in the same tradition appeared, Andrew Lang's *Prince Prigio* (1889)—which owes only the same kind of debt to *The Rose and the Ring* and the traditional fairy tales as Thackeray owed to his sources. In each case a writer of real genius was using, as it were, the same company and setting to put on a play of his own devising, and such as only he could have written.

Thackeray's indirect influence may, however, be traced in another original if somewhat controversial genius, George MacDonald, whose first children's story, *The Golden Key* (1861), was pure allegory in a setting only superficially that of any known fairyland, but who showed a strong dash of the comic Fairy Court tradition by the time he reached his third, *The Light Princess,* in 1864 (written two years earlier). After this he attempted longer stories, beginning with the full-length *At the Back of the North Wind* (1870, dated 1871) which combines dream, allegory, and fairy tale in a not completely successful whole, but reached his real heights with *The Princess and the Goblin* (1871) and its even better sequel *The Princess and Curdie* (1882, but serialized 1877).

Critical judgement of MacDonald's work is rendered difficult, as in the case of several writers with superlative powers of imagination which far out-run their skill as literary craftsmen. The classic example of this uncomfortable dualism is Rider Haggard, whose amazing imagination and narrative powers would place him among the truly great did not his woefully inept use of language and creation of character press him back amongst the very minor novelists.

MacDonald's deficiencies are most notable in his adult novels and least apparent in his *Unspoken Sermons* and the best of his children's books and imaginative works.

The quality of the *Princess* books to a child is that of a haunted house—but a house haunted by entirely good and desirable ghosts. They leave behind a feeling of awe and wonder, the excitement of the invisible world (we may call it Fairyland at the time, but it is always something more) coming within touchable distance: the door into the fourth dimension is situated in the places that we know best—we may chance upon it at any moment, and with the thrill of delight and excitement quite divorced from any fear of the unfamiliar. Though the stories are not memorable, the experience and its enriching quality remain vivid, and MacDonald's greatness is shown by the fact that to reread him in later life is equally rewarding and brings no sense of disappointment.

LEWIS CARROLL CHANGES EVERYTHING

Two excursions into utterly different realms of the imagination which appeared at much the same time as MacDonald's finest children's books have also this quality of an appeal that continues through life: *Alice's Adventures in Wonderland* (1865) and *Through the Looking-Glass* (1871).

Coming when they did, these two books revolutionized writing for the young. They captured the irresponsible fantasy in the minds of most children, and with it the unrealized urge towards rebellion against the imposed order and decorum of the world of the Olympians; but the capture was made by a writer of exceptional powers, a scholar in love with the richness of language and the devastating precision of mathematics. This seemingly inharmonious concatenation of elements produced two masterpieces, of which the second, being a little farther away from the spontaneous inspiration of oral storytelling, is the more perfectly integrated whole.

It is unsafe to attempt to get nearer to [Charles] Dodgson's sources of inspiration. There seems to be no doubt that he made up the stories on the spur of the moment, telling them to children who were supplying much of the inspiration while he told by the interruptions, suggestions, and criticism which are inseparable from composition in this kind. It is also true that on account of his stammer, from which he was only free when talking to children, Dodgson [writing under the pen name Lewis Carroll] was seeking an escape into childhood and thereby recapturing or preserving his own to some extent past the normally allotted limits. The result is what matters, and in this case it was two of the best-known, best-loved, and most often quoted books in the language.

Although 'Lewis Carroll' set free the imagination, he had

no original followers, though his imitators were legion—
'People are always imitating *Alice,*' complained [children's
writer and editor Andrew] Lang in 1895. In fact the only
writers to draw anywhere
near him in his peculiar
realm of fantasy, non-
sense, and felicitously
haunting turns of phrase
are Rudyard Kipling with
the *Just So Stories* (1902)
and A.A. Milne with his
two *Pooh* books in 1926
and 1928. One has only to
turn to Tom Hood again
(*From Nowhere to the
North Pole,* 1875) to see
how completely impossi-
ble it is to write a memorable imitation of *Alice.*

Perhaps because of this
impossibility, the last quar-
ter of the nineteenth century tended to produce
fewer and fewer examples
of the child's quest for the
'perilous seas' of fairyland

*This illustration appears on the
first page of Lewis Carroll's* Alice's
Adventures in Wonderland.

and concentrate with more and more skill on the presentation of childhood in the world of every day.

STORIES OF EVERYDAY LIFE APPEAR

This was the main theme of Catherine Sinclair's protest, but
its application was slow and tortuous. Superficially it was
not new, since Maria Edgeworth and Mrs Sherwood pro-
fessed to be writing about real children in their daily lives. A
distinct step forward was taken by Charlotte Yonge with her
novels for teenage girls, such as *The Daisy Chain* (1856), and
in the following year by Thomas Hughes in his outstanding
story of public school boys, *Tom Brown's Schooldays.*

Smaller children, however, were still being subjected to
the lachrymose-pious [tearful or preachy], as in *Jessica's
First Prayer* (1867) and *Misunderstood* (1869), though a
new writer first made her mark in the second of these
years, Juliana Horatia Ewing (1841–85), with *Mrs. Overthe-*

way's Remembrances. She progressed to *A Flat Iron for a Farthing* in 1872 (which year also saw Elizabeth Anna Hart's one outstanding child-novel, *The Runaway*), and reached her greatest heights with *Six to Sixteen* (1875) and *Jan of the Windmill* (1876).

The impact of these first outstanding child-novels is shown by Kipling's reference to *Six to Sixteen* in his autobiography: 'I owe more in circuitous ways to that tale than I can tell. I knew it (in 1875) as I know it still, almost by heart. Here was a history of real people and real things.'

Although Mrs Ewing may have had a better style, and on a small scale could produce better work, she was far surpassed as a child-novelist by Mrs Molesworth (Mary Louisa, née Stewart, 1839–1921). Although several of her longer books remain popular and stand up to rereading, Mrs Ewing is best remembered by her miniature novels, or long short stories, *Jackanapes* (1884) and *The Story of a Short Life* (1885); but their appeal is now more strong to the adult than the child, since they both turn on child-deaths which needs a conscious return to the days of high infant mortality on the part of the reader for any appreciation, and seem awkward and sentimental to a modern child. Though often derided, stories of this kind should not be condemned out of hand: Mrs Ewing's two remain classics, and they have close runners-up in Mrs Molesworth's *A Christmas Child* (1880) and Frances E. Crompton's *Friday's Child* (1889).

This was, however, almost the only death-bed in Mrs Molesworth's voluminous works for the young (two short stories and an opening chapter complete her list of early deaths; no parents meet their end during the course of any book, though a few endure dangerous illnesses, and only one child becomes a cripple). Her greatness lies in the fact that she was at once the faithful mirror of her own age and yet wrote, at her best, about the universal aspects of childhood.

It is no exaggeration to describe Mrs Molesworth as the Jane Austen of the nursery. Although her works are to Jane's as the miniature is to the great painting, such books as *The Carved Lions* and *Two Little Waifs* and *Nurse Heatherdale's Story* are as nearly perfect in their small kind as the great novelist's are in hers. Like her novel they are 'period' without being dated; they appeal to the heart as well as to the intellect; they remain in the memory and enrich the experience; they not only played an important part in their own branch of our literature but deserve an abiding place on our shelves to be read and reread by young and old.

Not only is one told in Mrs Molesworth's stories what it was like to be a child seventy-five years ago; as one reads one can experience all the hopes and fears, all the miniature loves and hates, passions and despairs, plots and counter-plots of that distinct, if rather restricted, little world. She truly understood children and could see life again with their eyes, and give vividness and poignancy to their small troubles in such a way that even to the adult reader the suspense may be as strong and as compelling as if it were a matter of life and death among grown men and women. So many of the basic problems and conflicts of life make themselves felt at all ages that this novel view of them back through the tele-scope into the eye of childhood seems in her best work to clarify and accentuate their relevance.

Although after such early stories as *Carrots* (1876) and *Hoodie* (1881) Mrs Molesworth avoided any hint of direct preaching, there is always a certain underlying intention in her stories. Well though she and such writers as Mrs Ewing and Mrs Hodgson Burnett understood children, they had not quite escaped from the tradition of the child as a miniature adult, as always in training for grownup life. This tends to make the children seem a little on their best behaviour, and it gives perhaps an undue emphasis to the continual mould-ing of character, occasionally an exaggerated importance to a small sin or backsliding. The children are just a little bet-ter than ourselves; to some extent the same is still true in such recent masterpieces as Arthur Ransome's stories of hol-iday adventures, but most of the conscious recognition of and combat with temptation has now gone. Acute introspection plays a relatively small part, however, in Mrs Molesworth's stories, though one told in the first person like *The Carved Lions* (1895), which is probably her masterpiece, gains greatly by the insight into the heroine's mind which it allows.

THE GROWTH OF INTROSPECTION

For more pronounced introspection we must turn to Mrs Hodgson Burnett, who wrote many minor works but only three which are on the definitely higher level which still makes them vividly alive. The first, *Little Lord Fauntleroy* (1886), suffers both from its intractable material—the balance without sentiment or patronizing between the democratic child of America and the aristocratic child in England—and from its unenviable reputation derived mainly from its translation into a stage sweetmeat for sentimental adults. Given a sympathetic reader who is ready to accept the limitations imposed by its period, the book is still remarkably readable both by young and old. Less difficult, though less

---

SUNDAY SCHOOL LITERATURE

In the eighteenth and nineteenth centuries, most children's books were distributed by the church with the intent to teach moral lessons and good behavior. The Marguerite Archer Collection of Historic Children's Materials has collected hundreds of these rare books.

Since children had few literary options in the early 19th century, publishers that distributed to Sunday schools began to fill the need for children's literature. Moral tales (didactic fiction), first written for children in the mid-18th century, became the predominant genre of literature for children. In many communities, parish workers distributed "reward books," or tracts designed to teach virtuous conduct.

Many examples of Sunday school literature depicting important aspects of 19th-century life are housed in the Archer Collection, including over 150 books published by the American Sunday School Union, an interdenominational organization founded in 1817. The Union produced works diverse in scope and content, such *as The Palm tribes and their varieties* (circa 1840s–1850s), a botanical work with extensive research on the geographic distribution of palms; *Learning to feel* (1846), an example of moral education that contains sections discussing every emotion; and *The Northern Whale-Fishery* (circa 1850s), on whaling.

Other publishers also produced notable Sunday school literature. *Cottage scenes, or, Stories of poor children and their parents* (Carlton and Porter, NY, for the Sunday School Union, circa 1860), discusses moral issues in relation to poverty. *The History of Adjal: the African slave boy who became a missionary* (Carlton and Porter, NY, circa 1850) is the biography of Samuel Crowther, who became a bishop in Nigeria. *Memoirs of Elizabeth Emory, daughter of Silas and Jane Emory, of Fulton, Oswego County, New York* (Lane & Scott, NY, for the Sunday School Union of the Methodist Episcopal Church, 1849) provides a realistic death account of a young woman.

Meredeth Eliassen, "From Dime Novels to Disney: San Francisco's Archer Collection Houses It All," *School Library Journal*, July 1995.

convincing to the adult, is her second major story, *A Little Princess* (1905—but a revised version of an earlier book published in 1887), which exploits the theme of the lonely child fallen from high fortune to poverty and persecution and then rescued at the eleventh hour by means which seem supernatural until satisfactorily explained at the end. The book is brilliant fare for children, but not one which weathers the test of adult rereading with complete success.

Her last book, *The Secret Garden* (1911), is one of great individuality and astonishing staying power. It is the study of the development of a selfish and solitary little girl later in contact with an hysterical and hypochondriac boy of ten: a brilliant piece of work, showing unusual understanding of introspective, unlikeable children with a sincerity that captures many young readers and most older ones.

Children with a country upbringing have found a similarly satisfying quality in *The Carved Lions,* with its less introspective and more sympathetic heroine, and Mrs Molesworth's less convincing *Sheila's Mystery* (also 1895), which deals not quite so happily with the salvation of one of her few unpleasant children. The significant difference is that while Sheila's solution is found for her by intelligent adults, Mary in *The Secret Garden* works out her salvation for herself—with the aid of an imposing array of coincidences. Between the writing of these two books another change had come over the child-novel and one of considerable importance; it seems to owe its main impetus to Kenneth Grahame's *The Golden Age,* also published in 1895.

THE IMPACT OF *THE GOLDEN AGE*

Now *The Golden Age,* undoubtedly one of the most important landmarks in the history of children's literature, is not a children's book at all. Misguided parents have frequently thought that it was: so far as I can remember *The Golden Age* was the only book which, as a child, I really and violently hated. The reason, curiously enough, seems to be that Kenneth Grahame knew too much. Here was an adult writing in an adult style about things which touched the very heart of our mystery; he was profaning the holy places—perhaps (for his manner was elusive) he was laughing in his detestable Olympian fashion at the things which really mattered.

The Golden Age, said Oswald Bastable in *The Wouldbegoods,* 'is A1, except where it gets mixed with grown-up nonsense.' Even E. Nesbit did not quite realize where the trouble lay, since she had never read it as a child. For to the older reader *The Golden Age* (with its sequel *Dream Days*, 1898) is, as Swinburne said of it, 'well-nigh too praiseworthy for praise': it is not merely one of the greatest books of its period, but a classic in its own right and an outstanding example of English prose.

Its importance in the present survey rests in its approach to childhood and its amazing understanding of the workings of the child's imagination and outlook. Hitherto the child had been pictured to a greater or less extent as an undeveloped adult, and all his books were intended in some degree to help force him into life's full flowering. Sheer instruction may have faded into the background, but an undercurrent of teaching in morality, in manners, in the sense of duty was always present. Even Mrs Molesworth never escaped from this background purpose, close though she came to the real thoughts and sensations of childhood—to the child looking forward to adulthood rather than the adult pushing the child into it. In the greater writers even the conscious push was not necessarily a blot: Mrs Ewing, Mrs Molesworth, and Mrs Hodgson Burnett could make of it a triumph as, in a completely different way, could George MacDonald.

But *The Golden Age* suddenly presented childhood as a thing in itself: a good thing, a joyous thing—a new world to be explored, a new species to be observed and described. Suddenly children were not being written down to any more— they were being written up: you were enjoying the spring for itself, not looking on it anxiously as a prelude to summer.

The immediate result was a loosening of bonds similar to that wrought by the outbreak into mere amusement of *Alice* thirty years earlier. It had a marked effect even on writers already well in their stride; even Mrs Molesworth, nearing the end of her literary career, found it impossible to resist the new elixir altogether, and at least two of her later books, *The House That Grew* (1900) and *Peterkin* (1902), have a gaiety and a youthfulness that sets them among her half-dozen best child-novels. As for minor writers, one has only to compare the sickly sentimentality of S.R. Crockett's *Sweetheart Travellers* (1895) with the adventurous boyishness of *Sir Toady Lion* (1897) to see the difference at its most extreme.

The oddest omission from the majority of earlier child-novels which Kenneth Grahame brought into the front of the picture was the imaginative life of children, and its importance to the children themselves. It had cropped up in several books written with more than half an eye on the adult reader, notably in Dickens's *Holiday Romance* (1868), Jefferies's *Bevis* (published as a three-volume novel in 1882), and in Mark Twain's *Tom Sawyer* and *Huckleberry Finn* (1875, 1884). But when it appears in the child-novel proper, as in the first chapter of Mrs Molesworth's *Two Little Waifs* (1883), it is merely incidental, or a means (as in *Hermy,* 1881) of starting a train of incidents. Not until *The Three Witches* (1900) and *Peterkin* could she make it the centre of her story.

THE MAGIC OF E. NESBIT

Grahame had many direct imitators, but only one broke away from imitation and produced great and original work, and that was Edith Nesbit. She had been a hack journalist whose ambition was to be a poet for nearly twenty years when, in July 1897, a series of reminiscences of her schooldays in *The Girl's Own* ran away with her when she came to write of her childhood games of 'Pirates and Explorers'. From this grew the idea of producing sketches or short stories of the *Golden Age* variety, but purporting to be written by one of the children concerned. Most of Oswald Bastable's earlier adventures were contributed to the *Windsor* and *Pall Mall* magazines, both intended purely for adults, and only in the autumn of 1899 did she revise and link them, with a little rewritten earlier material from *The Illustrated London News* and several of *Nister's Holiday Annuals,* as *The Story of the Treasure Seekers.*

A few reviewers took it as an adult book: 'Don't be content to read *The Treasure Seekers,* but give it also to children. They will all bless the name of Mrs Nesbit,' wrote Andrew Lang, who described the Bastables as 'perfect little trumps' and preferred them to the heroes of *Stalky & Co.* which appeared at the same time. He went on to describe it as 'a truly novel and original set of adventures, and of the finest tone in the world'.

Lang himself was of an older generation and could still not quite reconcile the apparent lack of a moral with a children's book about contemporary children. Albeit with a twinkle in his eye, he had looked for and found a moral in his own original fairy stories (just as Dodgson had done with *Alice,* many years after its publication) and could at least make excuses for the moral shortcomings of such traditional tales as *Puss in Boots.*

E. Nesbit, though she could lapse into sentimentality with the best, made the shift from conscious 'elevation' to unconscious improvement, substituting tone for teaching with the untidy impetuosity which characterizes even her best work. In the second Bastable compilation, *The Wouldbegoods* (1901), she even rounded on the moral tale, made a face at *The Daisy Chain,* and (apart from the one monumental lapse over the supposed dead Boer War hero) wrote her best non-magical children's book. Most of the Bastable stories were based on incidents or inspirations from her own childhood, and the thorough assumption of the child's outlook in the person of the narrator, Oswald, allowed her to use the joyous freedom and colloquial verve which carried the child-novel right out into the spring sunshine once and for all.

In the 'real-life' line she could not follow up her initial success: *The New Treasure-Seekers* (1905) already shows strain and self-imitation, and *The Railway Children* (1906) tends to lapse back into the sentimentality from which she was usually able to escape. Moreover, surprisingly few child-novels followed hers that win anywhere near the status of classics (apart from *The Secret Garden,* 1911) until Authur Ransome produced *Swallows and Amazons* in 1930.

Apart from achieving complete freedom, E. Nesbit's real claim to greatness lies, however, in her series of Wonder Tales. Short stories in the Fairy Court tradition accompanied the earlier Bastable tales into the world (they were collected as *The Book of Dragons,* 1900, and *Nine Unlikely Tales,* 1901) and she continued writing them, producing as many again over the next dozen years. The best of these would have assured her of a place not so very much lower than Thackeray and Lang; but by combining her styles and expanding her scope she produced eight full-length stories in which magic is introduced into family circles and surroundings as convincingly and prosaically real as those of the Bastables.

Magic to most children is only just out of reach: it fills their imaginings and informs their games. With the sure, deft touch and the rather pedestrian matter-of-factness which she knew so well how to use to advantage, E. Nesbit turned the games and the imaginings into actual events. 'Actual' is the key word; here she has never been equalled. She may have learnt how convincing magic can be, if strictly rationed and set in the most ordinary surroundings possible, from 'F. Anstey' (Thomas Anstey Guthrie, 1856–1934) of *Vice Versa* and *The Brass Bottle* fame; she certainly knew and admired Mrs Molesworth's blendings of fact and fantasy such as *The Cuckoo Clock* and *The Tapestry Room*—the Cuckoo and Dudu the Raven are close relations of the Psammead, the Phoenix, and the Mouldiwarp: but the total effect is, at its best, original with the originality of sheer genius.

Her mounting skill is shown in her first series of three, *Five Children and It* (1902), *The Phoenix and the Carpet* (1904), and *The Amulet* (1906), each better than the last. Then came perhaps her supreme achievement, *The Enchanted Castle* (1907), with a delightful new family, unexpected and most credible magic, and a really cohesive plot instead of the string of adventures in her other books. *The House of Arden* (1908) and its overlapping sequel *Harding's Luck* (1909) keep to the same high level, though the construction begins to falter; and then the decline comes, through *The Magic City* (1910) to *Wet Magic* (1913), after which she had written herself out.

OTHER MEMORABLE WORKS

The period ends sharply with E. Nesbit. But to follow out her career three notable writers have been shouldered aside, each authors of individual works of such recognized importance and popularity as to need no comment: Kipling with *The Jungle Books* (1894–5), *Stalky & Co.* (1899), *Just so Stories* (1902), and *Puck of Pook's Hill* (1906); Kenneth Grahame for that ambivalent masterpiece *The Wind in the Willows* (1908), an adult's book for children written by one of the few adults who could reenter childhood at will; and Beatrix Potter, the only writer for very small children to produce works of real literature which adults can still enjoy—helped perhaps by her inseparable and equally outstanding illustrations.

Finally, spilt over from another medium, comes *Peter Pan,* the essence and epitome of all that the writers of the Golden Age were striving to capture. 'It has influenced the spirit of children's books,' wrote Harvey Darton, 'more powerfully than any other work except the *Alices* and Andersen's *Fairy Tales.*' From its shores (the play has been revived every year but one since it began in 1904, and the book, *Peter Pan and Wendy,* 1911, is only a little less immortal) we may sail adventuring in I know not how many new directions, but to the

Never, Never Land we shall always return—led away for magic moments by the boy who wouldn't grow up, before turning refreshed and reinvigorated to seek those joys in the world of real men and women from which he was for ever shut out. For such, to all of us of whatever age, is the true message of the great children's books.

Edward Stratemeyer's Legacy of Series Books

Peter A. Soderbergh

In the world of children's literature, the series book has been a popular staple for over a century. Peter A. Soderbergh, the former dean of the College of Education at Louisiana State University, Baton Rouge, gives a fascinating account of the initial hostilities publisher and writer Edward Stratemeyer faced when he created series like Tom Swift, The Bobbsey Twins, and Nancy Drew. For many decades, librarians and teachers rose up against the books—calling them shoddy and sensationalist—even though children clamored for them. The tide changed slowly, but even today series books still have to fight for respect.

During the Progressive Era the question of the influence of urban-technological excesses on American children was of deep concern to parents, teachers, librarians, and social reformers. If children were the 'finest fruits of civilization' (to use Anthony Comstock's words) then the forces of seduction and spoilage had to be identified and controlled.

How character was formed had been a matter of great interest since the 1890s. It was a complex issue, but no true expert on boyhood or girlhood doubted that what a child read was a vital key to what he became. 'That the influence of reading on character is one of the most powerful is granted by every high-minded person . . . ,' the editor of *Journeys Through Bookland* stated in 1909. 'We are what we read.'

And what were the youngsters reading? Not the old nemesis of earlier days, the notorious 'dime novel'. By 1900 it had declined to a state of virtual invisibility. Not 'lewd' magazines and spicy gazettes. They had not yet been passed down into children's hands. What was left to inspect? The series book. It was everywhere, it seemed. Copies of *The Rover*

Excerpted from Peter A. Soderbergh, "Stratemeyer Strain: Educators and the Juvenile Series Book, 1900–1980," in *Only Connect: Readings of Children's Literature*, second edition, edited by Sheila Egoff, G.T. Stubbs, and L.F. Ashley. Copyright © 1980 Oxford University Press, Canada. Reprinted with permission from Peter A. Soderbergh.

Boys, Motor Boys, Bobbsey Twins, Frank Merriwell, Dorothy Dale, and *Dave Porter* proliferated in bookshops, department stores, and newsstands. Young people were collecting and consuming them by the tens of thousands. Reformers began to wonder: Were reports of the death of the dime novel premature? Was the 'literary pestilence' back, masquerading as a book? Some thought so. In a February 1900 review of two *Rover Boys* tales, *Literary World* noted that 'None of these books represents the highest range of reading for boys, but all approach the dime novel order.'

Who was responsible for this new 'vulgarization of children's books?' The writers of such material, primarily: Gilbert Patten, creator of *Frank Merriwell;* H. Irving Hancock; and Frank G. Patchin, for example. But one name stood out from his colleagues, the undisputed king of the juveniles: Edward Stratemeyer. As the Pittsburgh *Dispatch* observed in 1904, 'Everybody knows that Edward Stratemeyer is the most widely-read of all living American authors for boys.' Stratemeyer was the author of 150 juvenile books and the founder of a literary syndicate that mass-produced 700 series book titles. Although he died in 1930, the residue of his work still disturbs many educators a half-century later. How professionals have reacted to his books over the years says as much about American pedagogues as it does about the series book phenomenon.

SERIES BOOKS CAUSE MUCH CONTROVERSY

With the publication of *The Rover Boys at School* (1899) the modern phase of series book history began. Written by Stratemeyer, under the name of 'Arthur Winfield', the famous sequence sold six million copies before it expired in 1926. Stratemeyer also created *The Bobbsey Twins* (1904), *Motor Boys* (1906), *Tom Swift* (1910), *The Hardy Boys* (1927), and *Nancy Drew* (1930). Total sales of these five series alone approximate 125 million copies. He produced eighty-one distinct series in the period 1894–1930.

Early objections to series books concentrated on three features. First, the poor quality of the prose. In a time when the elevation of human thought and behavior were cornerstones of progressivism, the texts of series books were an affront. An editorial in the *Library Journal* of December 1905 asked: 'Shall the libraries resist the flood and stand for a better and purer literature and art for children, or shall they "meet the demands of the people" by ratifying a low and lowering taste.'

The second feature that evoked criticism was the series book's tendency toward exaggeration and sensationalism. Stratemeyer's fictional heroes and heroines, it was felt, were worldly, sly, and preternatural. The playful, polite, persevering juveniles in the older books by 'Oliver Optic' (William T. Adams), 'Harry Castlemon' (Charles Fosdick), and Edward Ellis had been transformed into globe-trotting, saber-rattling, wise-acreing rascals who out-foxed adults at every turn. Educators were appalled at this high degree of improbability. It was unreal, suggestive, and overstimulating. 'The chief trouble with these books,' one of Stratemeyer's adversaries (Franklin Mathiews) wrote, 'is their gross exaggeration, which works on a boy's mind in as deadly a fashion as liquor will attack a man's brain.'

Another annoying aspect was the assembly-line manner in which series books were being produced. Stratemeyer was the main offender on this point. In 1906 he organized his system into the Stratemeyer Syndicate. From his office on Madison Avenue (1914) he presided over a 'stable of hired writers' whom he paid to complete his plot outlines. Between 1904 and 1915 he was thus able to release forty-two new series, which included 214 separate titles. Attractively bound at fifty cents a piece, Stratemeyer's books were inundating the market-place. Such an overabundance of standarized inferiority troubled educators who knew that the inexpensive, provocative books capitalized on children's 'mania for collecting things'. How could the tide of 'cheap and vicious' fiction be stemmed? No one seemed to know. Orton Lowe, a school administrator, summed up the dilemma in 1914: 'The juvenile series—the hardest problem to handle. . . . The series is always "awful long," all of the volumes are cut to the same pattern, they are always in evidence, and they are equally stupid. . . . What shall be done with them?'

THE ANTI-SERIES CRUSADE

The first stage of the anti-series book movement covered the years 1900–17. Unfortunately it must be described as exhortative, unscientific, punitive, and ineffective. The best organized campaigns were mounted by the American Library Association, Boy Scouts of America, and American

Bookseller's Association, who kept each other informed and aroused. Classroom teachers and PTA groups joined the crusade irregularly.

In the final analysis most parties to the counter-series book movement resorted to name-calling, dire warnings, and other pressure tactics. The despised books were pronounced 'vulgar', 'pernicious', 'trashy', and 'injurious'. Series book authors were characterized as crass materialists, men of 'no moral purpose', and managers of fiction factories. Some of Stratemeyer's products (*Tom Swift, Motor Girls, Moving Picture Girls,* e.g.) were castigated publicly as samples of the current cancer. Throughout the attacks Stratemeyer proceeded with business as usual. Professional detractors did not disturb him often. He was fond of saying: 'Any writer who has the young for an audience can snap his fingers at all the other critics.' He snapped his fingers frequently in those days, and sales of his books grew with each passing year.

The First World War brought all lesser conflicts to a temporary halt. At the end of fifteen years the 'good book' forces had little to show for their pains. Collectively, *Tom Swift, Rover Boys,* and *Motor Boys* had sold 10 million copies. And how many of those had been passed from reader to reader? There were a number of reasons why the initial anti-series efforts failed to weaken the grip of the juvenile book on the popular imagination.

The educator-reformers moved on the fragile, nineteenth-century assumption that flat disapproval and informal censorship would shape mass opinion. They attacked a corporate process with moralisms. As missionaries they sought to convert people who felt no sense of sin. They attempted no serious research, preferring to protect rather than to study children. In their desire to sweep series books from library shelves they enhanced the popularity of the banished items. Most importantly, they seriously underestimated the degree to which the series book had become a cultural artifact since its origination in 1861. Many respectable citizens had fond memories of the books of their youth and could not be incited to condemn their own pasts. As one chagrined educator said at a November 1913 meeting of public school librarians, the series books were surviving because 'often they were the gift of father, mother, or Sunday school teacher' (all of whom should know better).

CHILDREN GIVE THE BOOKS HIGH MARKS

With one war settled, hostilities between the series book and its opponents resumed in 1919 and extended to 1931. During those post-war years the fortunes of Edward Stratemeyer and his 'army of ghosts' rose to new heights. Twenty-six new series were produced, among them being *Honey Bunch* (1923), *Blythe Girls* (1925), *Bomba* (1926), and *Ted Scott* (1927), not to mention *Hardy Boys* and *Nancy Drew.*

It is to their credit that educators in the 1920s attempted to quantify the nature of the problem Mr Stratemeyer and his peers had been causing for several decades. Research studies, informal polls, and random samplings were conducted to find answers to the questions: What is literary merit? What do children read? Why do they choose one item and not another? Underneath ran the basic issue: Why, contrary to our best advice, do children insist on reading series books? The results were predictable and exasperating. Edward Stratemeyer, of course, could not have achieved pre-eminence in the juvenile book field if he had not already known the answers.

A brief report of the findings of four surveys will suffice to recreate the tone of the period. Some of the studies confirmed what series authors and their publishers discovered in the 1880s. Arthur Jordan's review of *Children's Interest in Reading,* done at Columbia in 1921, proved that series writers still ruled the roost because they knew what appealed to boys (war, scouting, sports) and girls (home, school, fairy stories). In 1922 a Johns Hopkins study concluded that any given book's external appearance was a significant factor in children's choices of reading matter. The physical dimensions and complexions of the most-likely-to-be-chosen books, it happened, fit the series book perfectly.

The major undertaking of the decade was the *Winnetka Graded Book List* (1926). Over 36,000 teachers and 800 pupils in thirty-four cities were polled during the 1924–5 school year in an attempt to identify existent standards of selection, the elements of 'quality literature', and children's basic interests. Supported by the Carnegie Corporation and the American Library Association, the report elicited considerable interest and sold 3,800 copies by early 1927.

The result was both good and bad news. On the positive side, earlier findings on the correlation between appearance and selection were validated. The bad news (which was withheld for six months) was that the reading habits of fifth, sixth, and seventh graders were dominated by Edward Stratemeyer. *Bobbsey Twins, Tom Swift, Honey Bunch,* and others—'unanimously rated trashy' *a priori* by a select panel of librarians—received near-perfect interest scores from 98 per cent of the pupils. The experts were confused. The authors of the study cried out: 'Just what is "literary merit" anyhow?' Despite administrators' careful planning and coaching of the pupils, the series book came bursting through the experiment. Stratemeyer was not surprised. In June 1927, as the Winnetka list was fading into oblivion, he told a Newark *News* interviewer: 'I receive a great many letters from boys and girls who read my books. . . . It shows their hearts are with you.'

The period ended on a note of frustration. In 1930, 5,510 pupils were furnished 50,845 titles and urged by Pittsburgh educators to express their preferences. Once again junior high pupils voted for Edward Stratemeyer. They dutifully ranked the 'outstanding books' they had been alerted to, but they gave their clearest endorsements to *Tom Swift, Ruth Fielding, Baseball Joe,* and *Outdoor Girls.* Worse still, when I.Q. scores were correlated to reading choices 'about twice as many series were reported by the people with *greater* mental ability.' Nonplussed, the author of the study remarked: 'It would be interesting to find out . . . just what makes the SERIES such a favourite [with adolescents].' Florence Bamberger may have been correct. Ten years earlier she had decided that 'adults appear to estimate children's book preferences most inaccurately.'

THE BACKLASH CONTINUES AFTER STRATEMEYER'S DEATH

In May 1930, one month before the Pittsburgh study was completed, Edward Stratemeyer died of lobar pneumonia at his Newark, New Jersey home. Ostensibly, the sixty-seven-year-old 'champion of juvenile series writers' was gone. He left an estate in excess of $500,000 and a literary syndicate of momentous proportions. After several months of indecision his daughters, Edna and Harriet, decided to carry on the tradition. In November 1930 the main office was moved to East Orange, New Jersey, and the Stratemeyer syndicate was again producing 'good series books for boys and girls'. The physical demise of Edward Stratemeyer was a matter of record, but educators would discover that he had not departed their midst entirely.

From 1931 to 1960 all was relatively quiet on the series book front. The attentions on both sides were diverted sequentially by the Depression, several wars, and the expansion of the mass media. Educators were busy reacting to charges of myopia and unpreparedness between 1945 and 1958. Radio, comic books, pulp magazines, motion pictures, and the rise of television undermined the series book's veritable monopoly of leisure time. It was only a long truce, however. The irrepressible series book, while educators were preoccupied with the new scientism, issued an old challenge.

Between 1953 and 1962 the Stratemeyer Syndicate released modernized sets of *Tom Swift, Jr.* (1954), *Honey Bunch and Norman* (1957), *Hardy Boys* (1959), *Nancy Drew* (1959), and *Bobbsey Twins* (1961), and four new series, *Happy Hollisters* (1953), *The Tollivers* (1957), *Bret King* (1960), and *Linda Craig* (1962). Pedagogical reaction to the rejuvenation of the books was not immediate but when it did develop, it took two distinct forms. The more familiar of the two might be described as classical in mood and methodology. It was heavily populated by librarians, older teachers, English educators, and literary observers. In their statements one found attitudes identical to those expressed by their resolute antecedents of 1902–17. If they were not elitist (in that they, as adult experts, knew what was best for the reader) they were at least authoritarian. The classicists were loathe to relinquish the power of choice to the child, genuinely concerned he or she might linger too long on impoverished material. Their armory of weapons included verbal disapproval, printed criticism, and policies of exclusion.

Thus, in 1963, a respected educator, Dora Smith, wrote of Edward Stratemeyer and his 'hired hacks' who contributed to the 'tremendous spread of cheap, tawdry fiction, akin to the dime novel. . . .' In 1965 the American Library Association circulated recommendations to small libraries to aid in the elimination of *Nancy Drew, Bobbsey Twins, Hardy Boys, Tom Swift*, and other 'outmoded and poorly written series'. Dorothy R. Davis, a distinguished bibliographer, in 1967 held Stratemeyer responsible for the 'low regard' in which series books were held by 'persons in the field of juvenile literature'. In 1972 a recognized authority on children's books, Selma Lanes, used terms such as escapist, regressive, wooden, and banal with reference to *Nancy Drew, Hardy Boys*, and *Bobb-*

sey Twins. The librarians in the Stratemeyer Syndicate's home city of East Orange could not recall having a series book in stock since 1950. If children wanted series books they could 'get them elsewhere'. In 1978 the librarian of the Newton (Mass.) Public Library refused to stock *Nancy Drew* and *Hardy Boys* books on the basis of their poor literary quality.

THE TIDE FINALLY TURNS

In the mid-1960s an unofficial demurrer to the classicist position evolved. The developmentalists were a minority coalition of selected English educators, psychologists, and Language Arts instructors.

The developmentalists strove to direct professional and parental concerns away from a given enemy toward the particular needs of the reader. 'How to Get the Most Reluctant Reader to Read, Read, Read!' was the general battlecry. Recommendations were phrased in positive, unpatronizing language. The will to dictate and censor was absent. Debates on literary merit were forsaken as unprofitable. Parents and teachers were encouraged to view reading as a continuum, the reading habit as scrutable, and the various reading stages as identifiable elements in the total maturation process. The developmentalist attitude toward the series book was benign, as three samples from the literature indicate.

In 1966 a paper by John Rouse entitled 'In Defense of Trash' called for a revision of the abstractions formerly employed to measure literary quality. A good book, the author thought, could be one 'which gives the student a meaningful emotional experience.' Even a series book might do that, 'whether or not it is admired by the cognoscenti.' 'Teachers and librarians are sometimes too concerned with the quality of books . . . ,' an English educator, Dwight Burton, said in 1968. He referred to research that allowed that 'enthusiastic readers of mature works' had often consumed 'tons' of *Nancy Drew, Tom Swift,* and *Bobbsey Twins* material. In 1971 a 239-page guide for adults, *Books and the Teen-Age Reader,* contained a chapter on 'Subliterature'. Included was the series book—still inferior, but at least a member of the literary race. In fact, 'certain benefits' might accrue to the breathless reader of the *Hardy Boys.* Series books sustained the reading habit, perhaps. That their climaxes and endings were standardized might enhance the reader's sense of security.

It is likely that the series book will remain an anathema

to classicists who feel compelled to stand between the reader and low-level material. The developmentalists appear to have made a realistic (but cautious) accommodation during the 1970s to a fact of American life. They have chosen to expend their energies on the whetting of reading appetites among the young, letting the series book fall where it may. Neither group, of course, has faced the series book syndrome squarely. Both employ avoidance techniques—one tradi- tional, the other seemingly advanced. The questions raised by their predecessors of the 1920s remain unanswered. There is still an element of astonishment that the series book captures so many imaginations but no serious attempt to discover why it does. In a manner of speaking, the will of the masses has been treated, thus far, with disdain.

That the series book persists after eighty years of conde- scension and coercion is adequate justification for a defi- nite study of the phenomenon, but there may be other rea- sons as well.

During the [1970s] public interest in vintage series books increased visibly. Prices on works such as *Elsie Dinsmore* and *Frank Merriwell* have risen with the demand. Books written by Edward Stratemeyer under his own name are ap- proaching the status of collector's items, often commanding $7.50 per volume. More articles about the juvenile book tra- dition have been published since 1963 than in the forty pre- vious years. A number of university libraries (notably, Michigan State's) have sought to amass representative col- lections of series books from the 1868–1930 period. Tran- scending waves of 'nostalgia' and cyclical faddism, an awareness of the books' usefulness as a mirror of our former selves has been growing. Educators in many academic dis- ciplines might find the nature and function of series books worthy of consideration in the classroom. Certainly this genre of book ranks with those silent films, company cata- logues, and Edwardian periodicals we endorse as illumina- tors of the American character.

Opposition and apathy notwithstanding, the current se- ries book moves confidently toward 2000 A.D. If the record of the Stratemeyer Syndicate is an index, external negativity has had no demonstrable effect on its products. In 1979 *Nancy Drew* was purchased (by parents, for their children, as often as by the children themselves) at the rate of two mil- lion copies. The *Hardy Boys* and *Bobbsey Twins* sets sell one million and 250,000 titles a year respectively. Several series are available in foreign language editions. Syndicate books are well-received in Scandinavia, Great Britain, Italy, and Holland. *Nancy Drew* may be the most popular juvenile book in France. New series (*Winn and Lonny*) and modernizations of older series (*Dana Girls*) have substantial reader followings. By any standard, this is an impressive, ongoing achievement replete with implications for education.

Controversial though it may be, the ethos of Edward Stratemeyer prevails. It manifests when parents ask their local librarians why they do not make series books available to children. It manifests when an apprentice teacher wonders why her training program does not acknowledge the existence of books she collected and enjoyed. And it manifests in the thousands of letters children write to his syndicate each year, expressing their enthusiasms for the latest story. He would be pleased to know that, as he said over fifty years ago: 'It shows their hearts are with you.'

The End of the Idealized View of Childhood

Jackie Wullschläger

Jackie Wullschläger is a literary critic and feature writer with the *Financial Times* in London. Through extensive research on children's literature of the past century, she has found that modern children's books don't contain the idealized view of childhood and the child-centered universe found in Victorian and Edwardian classics like *Alice in Wonderland, Peter Pan,* and *Winnie-the-Pooh.* She attributes this to the social disillusionment of the postwar era, and on society's growing fixation with turbulent adolescence rather than innocent childhood.

A flabby bear; toys bought from Harrods [a department store in England]; the cosy Sussex garden: Milne tamed the fantasy, and in so doing heralded its destruction. After Milne, there were no more enchanted places in children's writing, and a tradition which had begun with [Lewis] Carroll's anarchic Wonderland in 1865, continued through [Edward] Lear's exotic tropical landscapes, [J.M.] Barrie's exciting Neverland island and [Kenneth] Grahame's English river-bank Arcadia to the safe rural idyll of Pooh, came to an end. The progression shows how the fantasy worlds of children's books gradually came closer to reality, until eventually the inventiveness of English children's fantasy ran out. Since *The House at Pooh Corner* in 1928, no world evoked in a children's book, with its own language, setting, tone, has entered the collective imagination and remained part of English culture in the way that Wonderland and the Hundred Acre Wood have done. With no children's characters after Milne's can one sum up a human type in a name—Piglet, Eeyore, the Mad Hatter, Toad—and be instantly understood. And no physical world in children's literature since Pooh's has been so immediately vivid, desirable, tangibly different: a self-contained alternative reality which is entirely convincing and satisfying on an imaginative level.

CHILDREN'S LITERATURE IS A REFLECTION OF SOCIETY

Why did Milne have no successors? At the heart of the matter lies the relationship between a society and its idea of childhood. For children's literature is a cultural barometer, revealing not only a society's idea of the norm of childhood—the portrayal of Alice gives a snapshot of a seven-year-old don's daughter in 1860s Oxford, Barrie's Darling children suggest a typical upper-middle-class Edwardian family—but its self-image and its aspirations. In Victorian and Edwardian England, childhood and the desire for purity were a key part of that self-image, and children's writers therefore expressed ideals and hopes and fears that were shared, albeit unconsciously, by much of their society. The result was the creation of an imaginative world and characters which still have the solid, lasting resonance of myth. Alice in Wonderland remains the archetype of any child or adult encountering the new and extraordinary; Peter Pan the eternal image of any person who does not want to grow up.

Both these characters are emblematic of the security and innocence of their times, both have a confidence untainted by cynicism. There is Alice's unshakeable belief that she can get by with good manners and self-discipline, and her priggish little self-admonishments ('Oh you foolish Alice!'). There is Peter Pan's boy-scout code of honour; his old-world chivalry ('And you a lady; never!', he says when he insists on risking his life to save Wendy); most of all his famous, patriotic 'To die will be an awfully big adventure'. In these aspects, both express the world-views of their creators and of their times. They belong to an age that was more innocent, happy to accept absolute values, less knowing and cynical and relativistic than our own. This intellectual security stands behind Wonderland, Neverland and all the enchanted, Eden-like places of the Victorian and Edwardian imagination.

THE END OF ARCADIA

The First World War shook this confidence irrevocably. England's national self-esteem and position in world affairs were fatally damaged and did not recover. Class hierarchies began to diminish; the thrifty middle classes received another blow with the collapse of the New York Stock Exchange in 1929. Never again could England look at the future with the certainty in the status quo of the Victorians. In 1918 Lytton Strachey satirised the hypocrisy and pomposity of nineteenth-century values in *Eminent Victorians;* in the 1920s Eliot, Huxley, and the radical, cynical, liberalising influence of Bloomsbury were the dominant voices. Carroll's idealisation of a little girl's virtue and good manners, Barrie's romance of honour and British courtesy and a stiff upper lip, belonged to a past age.

It is the post-war revolution in English society and culture that explains the decline of children's fantasies. Milne, a man obsessed with childhood and deeply involved with the childhood of his son, and a writer whose imagination was formed in the 1900s, was an obvious candidate to recreate an Edwardian Arcadia in the 1920s. Nostalgically, he recaptured the physical attributes of the old rural idyll, the escapism, the safe and unthreatened world of Edwardian England, but he could not win back the intellectual confidence, and this is why his books are shot through with mockery of the very idyll he was celebrating. He invented characters who lie and cheat, who are fearful and ignorant, who are self-doubting and confused, in a way that would have been poison to Grahame's upright, public-spirited river-bank animals twenty years earlier.

Winnie-the-Pooh is the only great children's fantasy not shaped by the social or sexual repression of its author. For by the 1920s, attitudes to sex as well as society were changing. The repressive moral climate which had made Carroll and Lear buttoned-up loners and Grahame and Barrie fearful and under-confident husbands was declining. Freud was writing about sexuality and the unconscious as a driving force in human behaviour and art at just the time when Barrie and Grahame were escaping from sex by writing their fantasies. Now Freud and the idea of psychoanalysis were beginning to be known. Sex was more open and

A.A. Milne and his son, Christopher Robin

widely discussed. There was less reason for adults to escape into a dream of childlike innocence, and at the same time Freud debunked the idea that a child *was* sexually innocent. The child was no longer an appropriate mirror or an ideal for a society: after the First World War, and especially during the depression of the 1930s, England was neither secure, innocent nor optimistic about the future. . . .

CHILDREN'S FANTASY GROWS UP

Children's fiction of course continued to be written, but nothing matched the energy and imagination and inventiveness of the earlier years. The children's books which have survived from the 1920s and 30s are predictable and plodding—the adventure stories of Arthur Ransome's Swallows and Amazons series and Hugh Lofting's Doctor Doolittle books; the imitation of Beatrix Potter in Alison Uttley's Little Grey Rabbit stories; Mary Poppins, the Peter Pan-like flying nanny who believes that 'everybody's got a Fairyland of their own'. The debt to the rural dream, the Neverland island, the fantasies particularly of Grahame and Barrie, are clear, but none of these works approached their literary quality or their element of myth.

Only [J.R.R.] Tolkien in *The Hobbit* in 1937, and *The Lord of the Rings*, written in the following years but not published until the 1950s, attempted a work which was original in spirit. He follows the great fantasies in the creation of a tangible, alternative reality, but there is something forced and self-conscious and intellectual about it, like an exercise in updating Anglo-Saxon chronicles (which Tolkien taught at Oxford), and it is perhaps for this reason that it has not entered English culture at the level of myth in the way that Toad and Badger or Pooh and Eeyore have. The world of the Hobbit is not Arcadian—Tolkien, who fought in the First World War, is more concerned with the nature of evil—and it was not created specifically for children; Tolkien's fantasies are enjoyed both by children and by many adults who never read them when young. They mark a transition between the time when fantasy was predominantly a genre of children's writing, and post-war literature, when fantasy became a popular adult genre used by authors as diverse as Angela Carter and Terry Pratchett. In a sense, adult literature has taken fantasy over, and adults now allow themselves the frivolity and poetry of fantastic, unreal places—perhaps because mainstream literature is less fanciful and sentimental than Victorian novels, and so escapist adult fantasies fill a gap.

A WELCOME RESURGENCE

In the 1920s and 30s, it was only in European children's literature, which emerged in the context of quite different social upheavals and questions of national self-identity, that a powerful and lasting mythical world was created. It has remained in Jean de Brunhoff's courtly, expressive Babar stories, which A.A. Milne persuaded Methuen to publish in English in 1934; in Antoine de Saint-Exupéry's *The Little Prince*—Saint-Exupéry was another children's writer who never really grew up, writing to his mother once that 'I am not sure that I have lived since childhood'; in Erich Kästner's *Emil and the Detectives,* where 1920s Berlin becomes a sort of intoxicating urban equivalent of the English secret garden. Unlike their derivative English contemporaries, each of these books is absolutely authentic in its relation to the culture of its times. Kästner, for example, is as close to German expressionist cityscapes as Grahame is to Arcadian paintings of the English countryside.

English children's literature saw something of a renaissance in the 1950s, significantly the modern decade when Britain was at its most optimistic and forward-looking. C.S. Lewis's Narnia chronicles, beginning with *The Lion, the Witch and the Wardrobe* (1950), Michael Bond's *A Bear Called Paddington* (1958), Mary Norton's The Borrowers series (begun 1955) and Philippa Pearce's *Tom's Midnight Garden* (1958) are all modern classics. The influence of the fantasy tradition on each of them is strong.

Paddington Bear is an updated Pooh with a dash of international glamour—he comes from Peru—though the Paddington books are not fantasies but homely stories about a London family where one child happens to be a comically inept bear. *The Borrowers* is an account of a self-contained fantasy world, this time of tiny people who live beneath the floorboards and 'borrow' from the property of those living above. Unlike its Arcadian predecessors, it is an ugly, claustrophobic world whose heroine Arriety cannot wait to leave it; her final escape into everyday adult life is the happy conclusion—the reverse of Christopher Robin's reluctant farewell to the world of his childhood. *The Borrowers* is a post-Freudian text in the way that *Winnie-the-Pooh* is not; beneath the sur-

face of the Borrowers' world is the tortured relationship between Arriety and her Borrower parents, who, amid protesta-
tions for her safety, try to keep her a child by preventing her
from going 'upstairs' to join the dangerous life of adults.

Fantasy is most powerfully an influence in *Tom's Midnight Garden* and in the Narnia stories. The first is the tale
of a long-destroyed secret garden which a 1950s boy discovers by entering the dreamworld of an old lady who was a
child in Victorian England; it is a superbly written and psy-

IN NO HURRY TO GROW UP

In The Literary Heritage of Childhood, *scholars Charles
Frey and John Griffith show that classic children's literature often elevated childhood's status to a level greater, and
more valuable, than adulthood.*

Antoine de Saint-Exupéry's *Little Prince* . . . opens with a thorough lambasting of adults and their ways. Grown-ups, we are
told and shown repeatedly, fail to understand children, love,
life itself. . . .

In *The Little Prince* and [J.M. Barrie's] *Peter Pan,* we are made
to feel that the end of childhood is the end of everything. . . .

[In Lewis Carroll's *Alice's Adventures in Wonderland*] Alice
begins her adult-mocking adventures at least partly out of
boredom generated by her older sister's pictureless book. To
grow is to gravitate into a world without images. When Alice
returns above ground, it is to a scene of "dead leaves," "dull
reality," and anticipated nostalgia for "the simple and loving
heart of childhood." Again, at the end of the second adventure
[*Through the Looking Glass*], Carroll invites us to mourn the
passing of childhood through a retrospective lament for the
way in which "Echoes fade and memories die: / Autumn's
frosts have slain July." It is a world of the "melancholy"
maiden's "unwelcome bed," as Carroll so pathetically puts it
in the *Looking-Glass* dedicatory poem which admits the
"shadow of a sigh" trembling through the story.

In Hans Christian Andersen's *Snow Queen,* Kay and Gerda,
who were initially led on their adventures by Kay's "mascu-
line" growth toward the mathematical world of icy reason, finally return home not to maturity but to be "children, children at heart." Many of Andersen's tales, of course, carry this
anti-maturational theme.

Charles Frey and John Griffith, *The Literary Heritage of Childhood: An Appraisal of Children's Classics in the Western Tradition.* Westport, CT: Greenwood,
1987, pp. 227–32.

chologically convincing book which depends for its resonance on images culled, consciously or unconsciously, from
Hodgson Burnett's classic *The Secret Garden.* Lewis is similarly derivative. In the Narnia books he makes a highly self-
conscious attempt to recreate an Arcadian idyll in didactic,
Christian terms. Wonderland and Neverland are his models,
but his own images and inventions are too unsubtle and intellectually controlled to work as symbol or myth.

ON THE SHOULDERS OF GIANTS

It is possible that we do not escape to Narnia or the Borrower
kingdom in the same way as we do to Wonderland or the
river bank of *The Wind in the Willows* because our imagination has already been caught by the children's fantasies
which have become established in the field earlier. English
children's books in the 1980s and 90s have continued to take
their themes and images and structure from their nineteenth
and early twentieth-century precursors, but, perhaps to overcome this, they offer a new twist. The best modern children's
writers, Roald Dahl and Janet and Allan Ahlberg, recognis-
ing derivativeness as perhaps inevitable, have made a virtue
of it by writing books which turn on post-modernist jokes
and revisions of established literary texts and conventions.
This is not quite as radical as it seems. Many of the poems in
Alice, such as 'You are old, Father William', are mocking revisions of worthy verses that Victorian children were expected to learn by heart, and Dahl and the Ahlbergs are thus
following a well-established anarchic tradition. Their joky,
inventive, highly contemporary revisions do, however, place
them in the post-modern tradition, and give them a cultural
authenticity which most children's literature since the Edwardians has lacked. This sense of being up-to-date probably explains their immense popularity and success as cultural reference points—a success all the greater because late
twentieth-century children are used to taking such references not from books at all but from television and film.

One of the Ahlbergs' most successful books is *The Jolly Postman, or Other People's Letters* (1986), where a postman delivers letters, which are physically extracted from 'envelope-
pages' in the book and read separately, to fairy-tale and
nursery-rhyme characters. The letters demand an extraordinary, street-wise sophistication from the child—the one to Mr
Wolf, from Meeny, Miny, Mo & Co Solicitors, on behalf of Miss

Riding Hood, threatens him with eviction from her grand-mother's cottage; the one to the Witch is a mail order cata-logue from Hobgoblin Supplies offering a non-stick cauldron set and gift ideas 'for the wizard in your life'. Children as young as four love this book; seven-year-olds who would now find the literary language and ideas of *Alice* impossibly com-plex are quite attuned to the cynical, adult nuances of legal and marketing companies. *The Jolly Postman* on the shelf next to *Alice* provides an instant picture of how expectations and images of childhood have become transformed in a century.

Dahl's stories, which are more literary and intended for older children, often turn on reversed expectations—a giant who is not evil but big and friendly in *The Big Friendly Giant;* a modern witch who is a headmistress in *Matilda.* Some of his characters are descendants of nonsense figures—the car-icatured child couch potato Mike Teevee who is stretched as thin as chewing gum after he has passed through a television screen; the greedy boy Augustus Gloop; the spoilt child Veruca Salt, disposed down a rubbish chute in *Charlie and the Chocolate Factory.* He could invent magical worlds—the chocolate rivers and minty sugar meadows in *Charlie and the Chocolate Factory,* for example—which seemed to emerge not out of nostalgia but out of contemporary children's lives. Dahl's books are original, compelling and anarchic, but he did not create a radical form of literature or a new vision of the world in the way that Carroll or Lear did.

SPOTLIGHT ON ADOLESCENCE

It is no coincidence that children's writers, in Victorian and Edwardian times among the most innovative literary talents, have since the 1930s been marginal literary figures, and that the original voices in English-speaking literature have for much of this century focused on the adolescent or youthful hero. In the mid-twentieth century, childhood, the epitome of innocence and security, was remote from everything English culture idealised and responded to. By the 1950s the romance with childhood was replaced by a love-affair with the adoles-cent or angry young man, a type much closer to the heart of modern Western culture, who represented what was turbulent and difficult, insecure and cynical, in sophisticated society. The Beatles, pop art, teenyboppers, were just a decade away.

In America, two teenagers, Lolita and Holden Caulfield, were the memorable literary characters of the 1950s, and

[Vladimir] Nabokov's *Lolita* and [J.D.] Salinger's *Catcher in the Rye* were both great works of literature and radical new departures in the art of fiction. In England their equivalents were Jimmy Porter and Jim Dixon, and again Kingsley Amis's *Lucky Jim* and John Osborne's *Look Back in Anger* were revolutionary in determining the future of the English novel and English drama. Where the Victorian and Edwardians had identified with literature's little girls and boys, Alice and Peter Pan, by the mid-twentieth century Holden Caulfield or Jimmy Porter were the favourite self-portraits of the reading classes. Now the fixation on adolescence has permeated popular fiction, in the same way that images of children permeated sentimental, popular Victorian fiction. The success of books like *The Secret Diary of Adrian Mole Aged 13¾* lies in society's adolescent self-image. And yet—there is still a child in all of us, and we return again and again, for comfort and enjoyment, to the children's books that emerged out of the Victorian and Edwardian love-affair with childhood.

The Birth of Realistic Young Adult Literature

Jack Forman

In the middle of the twentieth century, novels written expressly for teenagers began appearing, and by
the 1960s and '70s many of those books tackled serious issues in an unprecedented realistic manner.
Jack Forman, book reviewer and college librarian,
discusses the rise of the books which finally acknowledged that teenagers have different needs and
interests than younger children. The past four
decades have seen an amazing growth of books for
teenagers, and the genre continues to reinvent itself
according to the changing times.

In 1967 and 1968 three books were published that established the form of literature we now term the realistic young
adult novel or the problem novel—S.E. Hinton's *The Outsiders* (1967), Paul Zindel's *The Pigman* (1968), and Robert
Lipsyte's *The Contender* (1967).

Though these three novels clearly set the young adult
novel on a new path, they did not just appear "ex nihilo"
[from nothing]. They were an outgrowth of the twenty-year
post–World War II period when authors such as Henry
Gregor Felsen and Maureen Daly directed their storytelling
talents exclusively to the American adolescent. Felsen's *Hot
Rod* (1950) and Daly's *Seventeenth Summer* (1942), for example, were involving and inspiring junior novels geared to
the narrow and very special interests of adolescents as seen
by authors who reflected society's stereotypical views of
teenagers. For one thing, they believed that boys will be
boys—and girls will be girls; novels for males were about
cars and sports, and those for females were about dates and
dances. The world in which the teen characters lived seldom
extended further than the home and the high school, and the

plots dealt with the challenges the teen protagonists faced within this limited, white, middle-class environment.

While even the best of these novels were often didactic, they created sharply etched, highly individual characters with whom teen readers could easily identify. And, for the first time, they treated adolescents as entities with social and psychological needs separate from those of children.

During this same postwar period, another phenomenon took place that influenced the development of what we now call the young adult realistic novel. A small number of provocative novels, put out by trade publishers for adult audiences, filtered down slowly to the more sophisticated teen readers who found the junior novels too limiting and too remote from their everyday lives. These stories—such as J.D. Salinger's *Catcher in the Rye* (1951), William Golding's *The Lord of the Flies* (1955), and John Knowles's *A Separate Peace* (1959)—all possessed coming-of-age themes and youthful protagonists whose relationships with peers and the outside adult world highlighted moral and social concerns ignored by junior novels.

THE 1960S HERALD IN A NEW REALISM

By 1967 the teenagers of the 1960s had witnessed the assassination of a youthful, popular president and had seen the hopeful promises of the Great Society and of the newly created Peace Corps dissipate as a result of an uncertain war in Southeast Asia. They had also witnessed the bravery of many of their older brothers and sisters in Martin Luther King Jr.'s campaign of nonviolent civil disobedience against segregation laws, and they had seen the violent reactions to it. Television was thrusting the turbulence of the outside world into the relatively confined world of teenagers that Felsen and Daly had so effectively portrayed in their novels. In addition, rock music had matured into a creative form of expression that communicated the needs and aspirations of American teenagers in the sixties. Fewer and fewer teen readers believed that the worlds created by Felsen and Daly had any relevance to their own worlds.

It is therefore not surprising that the young adult novel would try to reflect some of the changes taking place in the sixties. Like the junior novels of the post–World War II period, *The Outsiders, The Pigman,* and *The Contender* were about teenagers and were directed exclusively to teen readers. And like the earlier stories, they attempted to deal with the social and psychological needs of the adolescent: social identity; personal identity; peer relationships; independence from family; and social responsibility. But the milieu had changed—radically. Bolstered by the surprising success of Salinger's, Golding's, and Knowles's novels among teen readers and influenced by the fast-moving and intrusive political and cultural events of the sixties, Hinton, Zindel, and Lipsyte moved the center of their fictional setting from the family and the school to places beyond—the street, the community, and the adult world.

In *The Outsiders,* S.E. Hinton wrote about a socially stratified high school society based not on personality differences but on socioeconomic backgrounds. The conflicts between the Socs and the Greasers were different from the ethnically stratified gangs of *West Side Story* (written in the early sixties) and from later stories dealing with youth gangs in the seventies and eighties. In *The Outsiders* one group (the Socs) represented the establishment and one (the Greasers) represented the "outsiders"; the Greasers' lifestyle, clothing, and families' socioeconomic background set them apart from the middle-class mainstream of the high school. Into this stratified setting, Hinton interjected highly individualistic teen characters who get caught up in a gang fight, with tragic consequences. Likewise, in Paul Zindel's *The Pigman,* tragic consequences result from the attempt of two disaffected teens to exploit the goodwill of a lonely old man whose wife has recently died. Here, however, the focus was not on what happens when teenagers are prisoners of social strata, but what happens when teenagers focus on satisfying their immediate needs at the expense of what they are doing to others. And with a more positive outcome, Robert Lipsyte's *The Contender* mixed the themes of personal success and social responsibility in a racially stratified setting that itself created pressures on a young and talented black would-be boxer.

The realistic young adult novel also parted company with the post-World War II junior novel in its refusal to accept gender pigeonholes. *The Pigman,* for example, has coequal protagonists—a boy and a girl who share the successes and the failures of their ill-fated relationship with Mr. Pignati. And, although *The Outsiders* is about boys, S.E. Hinton is female—and the story appeals equally to both genders of teen readers.

The characters in most post-World War II junior novels were white, Protestant, and middle class. The realistic young adult novel changed all that by developing characters with a wide variety of ethnic, racial, and religious backgrounds. The major characters in *The Contender* are black, Italian, and Jewish—representing an accurate microcosm of New York City, where the story takes place.

As these three novels quickly found acceptance with teen readers, more books followed that built on the strengths of this new genre. John Donovan's *I'll Get There. It Better Be Worth the Trip* (1969) dealt with a teenager, raised by his grandmother, who is forced to live with his alcoholic mother in New York City. Vera and Bill Cleaver's *Where the Lilies Bloom* (1969)—and its sequel *Trial Valley* (1977)—related the story of a gritty and tenacious Appalachian teenager, orphaned with her younger brothers and sisters, who struggles to keep her family together under adverse conditions. Glendon Swarthout's *Bless the Beasts and the Children* (1970) created a bond between five "misfit" children at a summer camp and a herd of hunted buffalo. *Go Ask Alice* (1971), published as a true diary of a runaway girl's involvement with street drugs and prostitution, was actually a fictionalized account based on a true story; the book shocked parents, teachers, and librarians because it was about a white, middle-class girl who, thirty years before, could have been the lead character of *Seventeenth Summer.*

CONTROVERSY AND HUMOR

Following the lead of the above-mentioned novels, other authors published books, but many did not meet the high standards established by Hinton, Zindel, and Lipsyte. In these inferior stories, fully developed characters became predictable stereotypes, imaginative writing and critical examination became clichés and pieties, and original plots were turned into derivative story lines. Even the later stories of Zindel, Hinton, and Lipsyte, all of whom wrote other novels in the 1970s, were vulnerable to these criticisms. But the 1970s also saw the publication of perhaps the most discussed and controversial young adult novel of the century—Robert Cormier's *The Chocolate War* (1974). It is an intriguing, gripping, and tightly written story dealing with a variation of "the outsider" theme: what happens when a lone teenager in a private school refuses to sell boxes of chocolate. When the teenager says no, he bucks not only the morally bankrupt leadership of the school, led by power-hungry, cynical Brother Leon, but also the intense and violent peer pressure of the established school gang that has been co-opted by the school administration to enforce its dictates. The reason why the novel was so controversial was not the cynicism of the school nor the violence of the gang but the story's pessimistic ending and ostensible message. "Don't disturb the universe," the physically beaten and spiritually drained teen rebel tells his one remaining friend. Parents, teachers, librarians, and even a few teen readers assailed this message of defeatism, but Cormier and his defenders claimed the novel was a description of the real world, not a prescription for passivity. *The Chocolate War's* controversial ending, however, highlights a major feature of realistic young adult novels: Like the best of adult fiction, the novels end celebrating the human spirit or depicting the depths of human depravity. *The Chocolate War* indicated that teenagers were no longer going to be protected from the dark side of life.

Nonetheless, many of these books emphasized the light at the end of the tunnel, often with humor and wit. Three of Walter Dean Myers's most popular novels—*The Young Landlords* (1979), *Motown and Didi* (1984), and *It Ain't All for Nothin'* (1978)—are about young teens in Harlem who transform their bleak inner-city environment into successful business projects, overcome their disruptive family lives while making close friends and falling in love, and turn street problems into adventurous challenges. M.E. Kerr's *Dinky Hocker Shoots Smack* (1972) parodies a mother who tries to do good for others but neglects her overweight daughter, and her *If I Love You, Am I Trapped Forever?* (1973) humorously shows the surprise and confusion of the self-proclaimed "most popular" boy in school when an unlikely nonconformist newcomer challenges his leadership role. Richard Peck, a former high-school teacher, wrote many successful novels about personal and social problems teens face, but three of his most popular stories—*The Ghost Belonged to Me* (1975), *Ghosts I Have Been* (1977), and *The Dreadful Future of Blossom Culp* (1983)—revolve around an unforgettable character named Blossom Culp, whose encounters with ghosts and other unworldly forms of life create some of the most down-to-earth and humorous situations in young adult fiction. Peck's imaginative satire of suburban life in *Secrets of the Shopping Mall* (1979) and his parody of beauty pageants in *Representing Super Doll* (1974) reflect the realistic novel's concern with societal issues even as it tries to entertain its intended teen readership.

THE BIRTH OF GENRE NOVELS

Between 1967 and the late seventies, the realistic novel constituted the mainstream of young adult literature. A serious challenge to the realistic novel's dominant position arose in the second half of the 1970s because of a decision by publishers to package fiction for teenagers in genre series in order to appeal to the interests and enthusiasms of young adult readers. This change in publishing strategy was a result of a variety of factors: the increasing success of the juvenile and young adult paperback market in retail bookstores; the influence of television and movies on what teens read; the realization that many teens were graduating from high school unable to read at the twelfth-grade level; and the success of the "hi-low" (high-interest, low-reading level) books packaged for this increasingly large group of young problem readers. However, although the genre packages that the publishers developed—such as "Sweet Valley High," "Sweet Dreams," "Wildfire," and "Confidentially Yours"—were initially profitable for publishers, they did not adversely affect the influence of the realistic novel. In fact, it could be argued that the realistic novel co-opted the genre stories.

The genre of sports novels, for example, combined sports action with predictable characters, who existed largely to make baskets, score touchdowns, or hit home runs—and to leave readers with hackneyed homilies and positive feelings. However, in the late seventies and the eighties when the genre packages were flourishing, well-written and provocative realistic novels with teen characters involved actively in sports were published for young adults. The function of the sports action, however, was not to drive the plot but rather to serve as a metaphor for the real action of the story that was taking place off the playing field. *Juggling* (1982) by David Lehrman, *Football Dreams* (1982) by David Guy, *A Passing Season* (1982) by Richard Blessing, *The Moves Make the Man* (1984) by Bruce Brooks, and *Running Loose* (1983) by Chris Crutcher are five of the best such stories, all of which featured teenagers whose athletic pursuits paralleled their life away from sports.

FOCUS ON ROMANCE

It is a far cry from the formula-driven saccharine plots of "Sweet Dreams" and "Wildfire," but many quality realistic young adult novels published during this same period dealt with teen romance. Robert Lipsyte's *Jock and Jill* (1982) mixed broad humor, a dash of politics, some sports action, and a lot of romance into a novel about love under even the most improbable of circumstances. Judy Blume's *Forever...* (1975) sketched a sexual love affair between two innocent teenagers that emphasized the humor of sexual activity and the impermanence of love. Harry Mazer's *The Girl of His Dreams* (1987)—a sequel to *The War on Villa Street* (1978)—was about a young high-school graduate who dreamt of the perfect girl to meet. *Annie on My Mind* (1982) by Nancy Garden sensitively portrayed a teen lesbian relationship that paralleled the physical and emotional aspects of teen heterosexual relationships. In all of these novels about love, romance was used as a backdrop in order to develop a rich, entertaining, unpredictable story peopled with colorful, complex unstereotypical teen characters to whom teen readers could easily relate.

RAISING THE BAR

In addition to enriching literature published specifically for young adult readers, the realistic young adult novel has raised the standards and broadened the parameters of all the fiction teenagers read. By successfully fighting the battles to tear down subject taboos and by introducing sophisticated literary devices and techniques such as foreshadowing, metaphors and similes, irony and allegory, and alternate first-person narratives and omniscient third-person narratives, the realistic novel paved the way for the quality contemporary adult novel to be considered desirable reading material for young adults. Among the more prominent of these novels were: Ernest Gaines's *A Gathering of Old Men* (1983), Chaim Potok's *The Chosen* (1967) and *My Name Is Asher Lev* (1972), James Baldwin's *If Beale Street Could Talk* (1974), and William Wharton's *Birdy* (1979), all of which were published originally for adult audiences. It is largely because of the influences of the successful, realistic young adult novel that serious fiction gained such a wide readership among teenagers.

During the past five years, one young Los Angeles novelist has emerged whose work promises to push the young adult novel into a very new direction. In four novels—W*eetzie Bat* (1989), *Witch Baby* (1990), *Cherokee Bat and the Goat Guys* (1991), and *Missing Angel Juan* (1993)—Francesca Lia Block has created a cast of memorable teen characters whose lives reflect a bizarre mixture of campy fairy-tale and punk reality. Her interconnected short novels are told in a richly lyrical and often allusive prose that portrays Block's sensitive but alienated adolescents as they make their way through L.A.'s often eerie and very real fantasyland.

What about the future of the realistic young adult novel? Rock music changed the direction of American popular music irrevocably in the fifties and sixties; although it has undergone changes of form and style since then, the core of the music is what it was at its birth. No one can safely predict the shape it will take in the next decade, but few are predicting its demise. Similarly, the realistic young adult novel changed young adult literature irrevocably in the sixties. Although it has changed forms and extended in many directions since then, it is as strong and influential as ever. It has made young adult literature honest, and it has kept the teenage reader honest. And the realistic young adult novel will probably continue to be the mainstream force in young adult literature, as long as it reflects life in a truthful way and keeps faith with the young adult's needs and aspirations.

CHAPTER 3

Common Themes of Children's Literature

Children's Literature

Subversion in Children's Literature

Alison Lurie

Alison Lurie is a Pulitzer Prize–winning novelist, Cornell University English professor, and author of a book of essays entitled, *Don't Tell the Grown-ups*. In this excerpt from the latter work, Lurie illustrates that many of the most beloved children's books contain elements of subversion and rebellion. Authors ranging from Mark Twain to Lewis Carroll to Dr. Seuss all infused their writing with elements that shook up the current establishment. In doing so, they earned permanent places in the hearts of their readers.

Imagine an ideal suburban or small-town elementary school yard at recess. Sunshine, trees, swings; children playing tag or jumping rope—a scene of simplicity and innocence. Come nearer; what are those nice little girls chanting as they turn the rope?

> "Fudge, fudge, tell the judge,
> Mama has a baby.
> It's a boy, full of joy,
> Papa's going crazy.
> Wrap it up in toilet paper,
> Send it down the elevator."

Soon the school bell will sound and the children will file into assembly. Gazing up at the American flag on the stage, they will lift their young voices in patriotic song:

> "My country's tired of me,
> I'm going to Germany,
> To see the king.
> His name is Donald Duck,
> He drives a garbage truck,
> He taught me how to – – – –.
> Let freedom ring."

Adults who have forgotten what childhood is really like may be shocked by these verses; but anyone who has recently read *Tom Sawyer, Alice's Adventures in Wonderland,* or any of a number of other classics should not be surprised. Most of the great works of juvenile literature are subversive in one way or another: they express ideas and emotions not generally approved of or even recognized at the time; they make fun of honored figures and piously held beliefs; and they view social pretenses with clear-eyed directness, remarking—as in [Hans Christian] Andersen's famous tale—that the emperor has no clothes.

MARK TWAIN'S REACTION TO GOODY-GOODY BOOKS

Mark Twain's *Tom Sawyer,* for instance, is not the kind of story contemporary authorities recommended for children. It was in fact written in irritable reaction against what Twain described as "goody-goody boys' books"—the improving tales that were distributed in tremendous numbers by religious and educational institutions in nineteenth-century America. The standard plot of such works was that known to folklorists as "Kind and Unkind." It is perhaps most familiar to us from Hogarth's series of prints depicting the lives of the Good and Bad Apprentices, the former of whom practices every virtue and rises to riches and honor, while his lazy, thieving companion dies penniless.

In *Tom Sawyer* Twain deliberately turned this plot on its head. Tom lies, steals, swears, smokes tobacco, plays hooky, and wins a Sunday school prize by fraud. He sneaks out of his house at night and runs away for days, driving his aunt Polly almost to despair. He ends up with a small fortune in gold, the admiration of the whole town, and the love of Becky Thatcher—while his goody-goody brother Sid is last seen being literally kicked and cuffed out the door.

Twain's portrait of his hometown, Hannibal, Missouri (which appears in the book as St. Petersburg), is equally seditious. Its adult citizens are shown as petty, credulous, and overawed by wealth, and their most respected local institutions are empty shams. The Temperance Tavern shelters thieves and outlaws, and sells whiskey in its back room. Church is a place of excruciating weekly boredom where "the choir always tittered and whispered all through service" and the entire congregation is delighted when the sermon is disrupted by a yelping dog. School is even worse: the teacher is a small-time tyrant who shames and beats his students while laboriously training the more docile ones to re-

A depiction of Mark Twain's controversial character Tom Sawyer.
When readers criticized Tom's deviant and unruly behavior, Twain
claimed that the book was meant to entertain children, not teach
them values.

cite bad poetry and even worse original compositions.

How, especially in 1876, did Twain get away with it? Partly
of course because he was a genius; but partly too because,
as he declared in his preface, *Tom Sawyer* was "intended
mainly for the entertainment of boys and girls," that is, not
to be taken seriously. *Huckleberry Finn,* which was issued

without this assurance, ran into trouble at once: it was called "vulgar" and "coarse" by critics and banned by the Concord Library in Massachusetts.

LEWIS CARROLL'S "UNDERGROUND" POLITICS

The greatest British juvenile author of the late nineteenth century, Lewis Carroll, was just as subversive as Twain, but in a more subtle way: it is appropriate that the original title of his first children's book should have been *Alice's Adventures Underground.* Modern critics have tended to see Carroll's heroine as exploring the inner world of the unconscious; but it is also possible to read *Alice's Adventures in Wonderland* and *Through the Looking-Glass* as underground literature in the social and political sense. The Walrus and the Carpenter have been described as caricatures of the rival politicians Benjamin Disraeli and William Gladstone, united in deceiving and devouring the innocent oysters, or voters, but in different styles. (This—at first sight farfetched—interpretation is given weight by Sir John Tenniel's illustrations, in which the Walrus sports Disraeli's elegant dress and luxuriant mustache, while the Carpenter has the square jaw and untidy clothes of Gladstone.)

The courts of the Queen of Hearts and the Red Queen, with their pompous formality and arbitrary laws of etiquette, can easily be seen as a grotesque version of the very proper and formal court of Queen Victoria, who also surrounded herself with extensive rose gardens and bowing courtiers. The King of Hearts, like Prince Albert, takes second place to his consort, while the Red King and the White King, though essential to the chess game upon which *Through the Looking-Glass* is based, hardly appear at all.

Carroll, unlike most of his contemporaries, was by no means awed by Queen Victoria. After *Alice's Adventures in Wonderland* had made him famous, the queen graciously signified through an intermediary that he might dedicate his next book to her. Carroll followed the letter rather than the spirit of this request, which was equivalent to a royal command: his next book, *Some Considerations on Determinants,* by Charles Dodgson, tutor in Mathematics of Christ Church, Oxford, was duly inscribed to Queen Victoria. *Through the Looking-Glass,* as it should have been, was dedicated to Alice Liddell, to whom the story had originally been told.

As one might expect from an Oxford don, the most thoroughgoing satirical attacks in the Alice books are directed at education. All the adults, especially those who resemble governesses or professors, are foolish, arbitrary, cruel, or mad. The only wholly decent and sensible person is Alice herself.

The Caterpillar, like a Victorian schoolmaster, asks unanswerable questions and demands that Alice repeat nonsense verses. Humpty-Dumpty, in the manner of some professors, asserts that he "can explain all the poems that ever were invented—and a good many that haven't been invented just yet." He also manipulates statements to suit himself ("When *I* use a word . . . it means just what I choose it to mean"). The Red Queen, like a mad governess, puts Alice through a nightmare oral exam ("What's one and one and one and one and one and one and one and one and one and one?"). The books are full of parodies of the moral verses found in contemporary school readers and of the rote question-and-answer method of teaching. The "regular course" of instruction followed by the Mock Turtle includes Ambition, Distraction, Uglification, and Derision, while the Gryphon goes to "the Classical master" to study Laughing and Grief: all the subjects that a child in the nineteenth century—or today—must learn in order to grow up and enter the adult world that Carroll hated.

Most radical of all at the time, though difficult to appreciate now, is the unconventional character of Alice herself. Except for her proper manners, she is by no means a good little girl in mid-Victorian terms. She is not gentle, timid, and docile, but active, brave, and impatient; she is highly critical of her surroundings and of the adults she meets. At the end of both books she fights back, reducing the Queen of Hearts' court to a pack of playing cards and the Red Queen to a kitten, crying "Who cares for *you*?" and "I can't stand this any longer!"

Both Twain and Carroll were split personalities in the social if not the technical sense of the term. As Samuel Clemens, Twain was a sentimental bourgeois paterfamilias, a would-be industrial magnate (he financed the manufacture of a typesetting machine that lost fifty thousand dollars) and a pillar of the community. Under the name Mark Twain he was a restless adventurer and a bitterly sardonic critic of the proper world his other self inhabited. "All the details of 'civilization' are legitimate matters for jeering," he wrote. "It is made up of about three tenths of reality and sincerity, and seven tenths of wind and humbug." Charles Dodgson the Oxford don was prim, devout, obsessive, and painfully shy; occasionally he even refused to accept mail addressed to Lewis Carroll, the affectionate and witty friend of little girls. . . .

SIDING WITH THE REBEL

Many other authors of juvenile classics, though not so . . . strikingly divided in personality as Twain and Carroll, have had the ability to look at the world from below and note its less respectable aspects, just as little children playing on the floor can see the chewing gum stuck to the underside of polished mahogany tables and the hems of silk dresses held up with safety pins. The instinctive sympathy of such writers is often with the rebel, the defier of social laws.

Toad in Kenneth Grahame's *The Wind in the Willows,* for instance, is foolish, rash, and boastful as well as incorrigibly criminal—a kind of Edwardian upper-class juvenile delinquent, with a passion for flashy clothes and fast cars. Yet at the end of the book, only slightly chastened, Toad is restored to his ancestral home and given a triumphal banquet by his loyal friends. Grahame, who was a secretary of the Bank of England, lived a quiet and respectable life, but it is hard not to suspect that in imagination he was at least partly on the side of "Toad, the motor-car snatcher, the prison-breaker, the Toad who always escapes!" . . .

Opinions and attitudes that are not currently in style in the adult world often find expression in children's books of the time. . . . During World War II, when "pacifist" was a dirty word, one of the most popular picture books for American children was Munro Leaf's *The Story of Ferdinand.* It is the tale of a gentle, noncombative—though very large and strong—bull who lives in Spain. All the other bulls "would fight each other all day. . . . butt each other and stick each other with their horns. . . . But not Ferdinand." What he wants is to sit quietly under a tree and smell flowers. Taken to the bullring in Madrid, Ferdinand steadfastly refuses to fight and finally has to be sent home again, where he lives happily ever after. (According to experts, this cheerful ending would be unlikely in reality; insufficiently aggressive bulls are usually killed in the ring. And, of course, conscientious objectors in World War II often went to jail—but one can dream.)

In some famous children's books, the subversive message

operates in the private rather than the public sphere. More or less openly, the author takes the side of the child against his or her parents, who are portrayed as at best silly and needlessly anxious, at worst selfish and stupid. In James Barrie's *Peter Pan*, Mrs. Darling is charming but light-headed, while Mr. Darling is a bully and a hypocrite. In *Winnie-the-Pooh*, as we shall see, the adults who surround Christopher Robin are reduced to the status of stuffed toys.

Mr. and Mrs. Banks, the parents in P.L. Travers's *Mary Poppins*, are helpless and incompetent at managing their own household without the help of their magical nanny. At the start of *Mary Poppins Comes Back*, things have gotten so bad that they are on the verge of separation: "'I don't know what's come over this house,' Mr. Banks went on. 'Nothing ever goes right—hasn't for ages! . . . I am going!' he said. 'And I don't know that I shall ever come back.'"

Mrs. Banks, exhausted, sits on the stairs weeping while the servants (the Bankses are only middle-class, but this is 1935) drop trays of china and set the kitchen chimney on fire and the children scream and squabble in the nursery. When their mother's misery and helplessness are called to their attention, their reaction is cool and detached:

> "Children! Children!" Mrs. Banks was wringing her hands in despair. "Be quiet or I shall Go Mad!"

> There was silence for a moment as they stared at her with interest. Would she really? They wondered. And what would she be like if she did?

Throughout the four volumes, it is clear that the children's real loyalty is to Mary Poppins.

THE ICONOCLASTIC WIZARD OF OZ

Of course, not all famous children's literature is wholly subversive. . . . L.F. Baum's *The Wonderful Wizard of Oz* . . . contains no sweeping criticism of the status quo, even though Baum, as a failed South Dakota newspaper editor, must have been well acquainted with the hard times, low farm prices, and rise in freight rates that had ground down prairie families like Dorothy's. Instead, geography and climate are blamed for the fact that Aunt Em, once a "young, pretty wife," is "thin and gaunt, and never smiled, now" while Uncle Henry "worked hard from morning till night and did not know what joy was."

The Wizard of Oz himself, however, combines the appearance of a Gilded Age politician with that of a medicine-show huckster, and in the central episode Dorothy and her friends expose him as a humbug whose powers and promises are as full of hot air as the balloon that eventually carries him back to Omaha. Baum is partially sympathetic to his hero, who as he says himself is "really a very good man" though "a very bad Wizard." He allows the Wizard to give the Scarecrow a brain, the Cowardly Lion courage, and the Tin Woodman a heart— or rather, by a sort of benevolent hocus-pocus, to convince them that they are receiving what they already obviously have. The implication is that there is a place in American society for the self-improvement merchant, even if his magic is mere deception. It was an iconoclastic message at the time, but one that has since been upheld by hundreds of American politicians and by entrepreneurs of Wisdom, Confidence, and Self-Realization from Dale Carnegie to Shirley MacLaine. . . .

L.F. Baum did not approve of everything about his country. The social historian Henry M. Littlefield has pointed out that Baum divided Oz into four kingdoms, of which two, the Gillikin Country in the north and the Quadling Country in the south, are ruled by good witches when Dorothy arrives—perhaps reflecting Baum's conscious or unconscious belief that Middle America was in fairly good shape. The Munchkins in the east, on the other hand, are ruled by a Wicked Witch, and she has transformed the originally human Woodman into a mechanical man who feels as if he has no heart—possibly a comment on the increasing industrialization and dehumanization of the eastern United States. As for the largely unsettled Winkie Country in the west, it is also dominated by a Wicked Witch, who threatens Dorothy and her friends with natural rather than mechanical dangers. Her attacking forces of wolves, crows, and bees may represent the danger to early settlers and farmers from wild animals, birds, and crop-destroying insects; and her Winged Monkeys, according to Mr. Littlefield, are Plains Indians.

MELLOWING WITH AGE

Time and social change mute the revolutionary message of some children's classics. After more than a hundred years, Jo March of *Little Women* no longer seems so radical a tomboy: her untidiness, literary ambition, enthusiasm for "romps," and mild boyish slang ("Christopher Columbus!") appear tame. Her later career as a writer of Gothic thrillers and the director, with her husband, of a partially coeducational boarding school does not have the thrill it once did. Girls who love Louisa May Alcott's books today tend to be rather more quiet, feminine, and domestic than the average. But for at least five generations of American girls, Jo was a rebel and an ideal, and Louisa May Alcott's understanding of their own impatience with contemporary models of female behavior ("I hate affected, niminy-piminy chits!" as Jo puts it) nothing less than miraculous.

In the second half of this century, as feminism launched its second wave, the limits of socially acceptable behavior for girls were steadily pushed back, and one "subversive" book after another was at first condemned and then applauded. When it first appeared, in 1964, Louise Fitzhugh's *Harriet the Spy* was criticized because its heroine secretly observed and dispassionately recorded the foolish behavior of adults. Its sequel, *The Long Secret* (1965), was censured because, for the first time in juvenile literature, it mentioned menstruation. Now both books are widely recommended. Astrid Lindgren's *Pippi Longstocking* was widely criticized when it was published in Sweden, in 1945. Today Pippi, who is careless of her appearance, mocks the school system, and can lick the circus strong man in a wrestling match, is an international favorite.

Dr. Seuss and Hidden Flights of Fancy

It is the particular gift of some writers to remain in a sense children all their lives: to continue to see the world as boys and girls see it and to take their side instinctively. One author who carries on this tradition in contemporary America is Dr. Seuss, who like Twain and Carroll has adopted a separate literary personality (under his real name, Theodor Geisel, he has been an editorial cartoonist, advertising artist, and screenwriter). Seuss's picture books, though extremely popular with children, have yet to be recognized as classics; they are not even mentioned in many surveys of the "best" children's books. Seuss is in good company here: *The Wonderful Wizard of Oz* was similarly neglected for more than fifty years, and Maurice Sendak's brilliant *Where the Wild Things Are*—which suggests that children sometimes have violent, aggressive impulses toward their parents—was at first condemned as "too frightening" (frightening for whom? one wants to ask).

From *And to Think That I Saw It on Mulberry Street* (1937) onward, Dr. Seuss has not only celebrated the power and richness of the child's imagination but suggested that children may do well to conceal their flights of fancy from their elders. The boy and girl in his best-known book, *The Cat in the Hat,* shut indoors on a rainy day, completely wreck the house with the help of the devilish-looking Cat, then tidy it up again just before their mother gets home to ask:

> "Did you have any fun?
> Tell me. What did you do?"
>
> And Sally and I
> Did not know what to say.
> Should we tell her the things
> That went on there that day?
>
> Should we tell her about it?
> Now, what should we do?
>
> Well . . . What would YOU do
> If your mother asked you?

The implication is that Mother will never find out what went on in her absence—and just as well, too.

Grown-ups reading this story aloud may feel uneasy; we prefer to think of children as ingenuous and confiding. Usually, too, we like to believe that everything is all right in our immediate world and that the opinions and attitudes expressed in the popular media represent the full range of possible opinions and attitudes. But if by chance we should want to know what has been censored from establishment culture in the past, or what our kids are really up to today, we might do well to look at the classic children's books and listen to the rhymes being sung on school playgrounds.

Children's Horror: A World Accustomed to Violence

Roderick McGillis

The 1990s saw a huge explosion of horror novels for children of all ages. Books that revolve around terror and murder are overflowing bookstore shelves. Roderick McGillis, writer and editor of many books on children's literature theory, studies a wide-ranging sample of these books to figure out how the authors weave their web of fear. He uncovers commonly-used plot devices and stereotypical characters, and concludes that these books—though obviously appealing to young readers—lead children to believe the world is full of hate, materialism, abuse, and violence.

I begin with a quotation from *Silent Stalker* (1993), a novel by Richie Tankersley Cusick, one of many contemporary authors writing novels of terror for young readers. The passage I have selected deals with a young girl named Jenny and a boy named Derrick, who claims to be protecting her from his mad twin brother, Malcolm. In actual fact, however, Malcolm and Derrick have another brother, Edwyn. The brothers are triplets, and Edwyn is the insane one. In the passage, Jenny and Derrick are in the depths below a typically European Gothic castle somewhere in the United States. As we might expect, Europe stands for decadence, perversion, torture, and even madness in the North American imagination. As Derrick, who in reality is Edwyn, leads Jenny deeper into the dungeons of the castle, he speaks of Malcolm:

> His grip tightened, and he pressed Jenny tenderly against him.
>
> "He fell in love with you, you know," Derrick said quietly. "That very first night. That very first time . . . he touched you—"

Excerpted from Roderick McGillis, "'Terror Is Her Constant Companion': The Cult of Fear in Recent Books for Teenagers," in *Reflections of Change: Children's Literature Since 1945*, edited by Sandra L. Beckett. Reprinted with permission from Greenwood Publishing Group, Inc., Westport, CT.

"Please don't," Jenny murmured. "Derrick, what are we going to do?"

"Ssh . . . you're safe now. Safe with me. . . ."

And then another dark place, darker even than before, Jenny could sense it and see it all at the same time, and she was being lowered down, down by her arms, down onto a cold wet floor, and it smelled of mildew and damp, and she could hear . . . *water?*

The rain . . . it's the rain I hear—the terrible storm—

Yet in the back of her mind she knew it wasn't the storm— no thunder—no lightning—just the thick, restless slurp of water. . . .

"Where are we?" she asked, and she was even colder now, something prickling along her skin . . . up her spine . . . filling her heart with sudden fear—"Derrick, where *are* we?"

Groggily she looked up. She could see the spurt of a candle, and she could see Derrick's face, but it seemed so far above her, everything miles and miles above her. . . .

Derrick looked down and smiled. The candlelight cast nervous shadows over his calm, calm face.

"We're in a secret place," he murmured. "Our secret. Yours and mine."

"Derrick—"

"In fact, it's so secret, nobody ever leaves here. Did I forget to tell you that?"

Many aspects of this passage are typical of similar books for teenage readers. A forced inconsistency in the writing amounts to overwriting: Derrick tightens his grip, yet he holds Jenny tenderly; water "slurps" rather than laps or flows or some other less indelicate descriptor. A young female finds herself the object of another's domination and manipulation: here Jenny is manipulated by Derrick (Edwyn, remember), who lowers her onto a wet floor. The female victim appears consistently in these books. Jenny's clarity and grogginess, tightness and tenderness are examples not only of inconsistent writing, but also of paradox to create tension. Also intensifying the situation are the italicized thoughts of one of the characters, here Jenny. Despite these attempts to create fear, the author asserts the feelings of fear as much as she shows them ("filling her heart with sudden fear"). And finally, the situation is familiar: a young girl finds herself in danger, separated from family and unsure of who near her might be a friend and who might be an enemy. The girl is a victim, and her victimization includes a frisson that is clearly sexual, in this case unpleasantly so.

THE FEMALE VICTIM

Often the girls in these books find themselves cut off from familiar spaces: in dark forests, on strange and exotic islands, alone in large houses, alone in empty buildings, alone at the beach, alone in the gym, alone at the lake, alone in a country phone booth, alone just about anywhere once the sun goes down, or alone in sinister Gothic castles, as in *Silent Stalker.* Often they are helpless; they require the assistance of a comforting and capable male. And because the male is comforting as well as capable, a titillation seeps into these books. Truly something creepy this way comes. For me, the most telling moment in the passage above occurs when Jenny sees "the spurt of a candle." Readers of Bram Stoker's *Dracula* (1894) might recall the moment in that book when three strong men violate the coffin of Lucy Westenra. As they force open the coffin, their candles drip "semen" onto the lid, reminding us just what is actually taking place here. Violation is common to books that draw on the sex-death instinct. Something in these books speaks to the instinct Freud discerned in all of us that turns toward sex and death. What could be more transgressive than vicariously experiencing this deeply disturbing and disturbed conflation of death and sex?

In case you doubt my reading of "the spurt of a candle," take a glance at several other suggestive passages in the book: "She could feel his body, tall and strong against her back," "Malcolm's heart was beating beneath her cheek, warm and solid," "eyes creeping over her," "raked Jenny from head to foot with his eyes," "so careful with her, so gentle with her." One of the characters in the book is an abused female named Nan (perhaps alluding to Oliver Twist) who remarks about the man she loves: "I take care of him. Even when he hurts me. Even when I know that someday he'll—." And yes, she dies at the hand of the murderer. Female characters are constantly the object of someone's gaze, someone hiding in the shadows, sometimes breathing audibly, watching. The repeated line in R.L. Stine's Babysitter books (so far there are four of these in print) says it all: "Hi, Babes. Are you all alone? Company's coming." Jenny, in *Silent Stalker,* experiences unspeakable torture in the fantastic Gothic structure to which her father has brought her, and nothing should be worse than enduring the probing, prying eyes of the stalker of the title. In fact, however, one character remarks to her that she "might be surprised how enjoyable some tortures could be." It might be horrific to be the object of someone's gaze, but it is also fascinating.

Silent Stalker might be an extreme example of a kind of writing adolescents find remarkably appealing, but it is by no means unique. In fact, horror books for adolescent readers have proven so popular that versions of the horror story are now appearing for readers from seven to eleven. Any number of series for young readers now exist: Fear Street, The Power, Blood and Lace, Goosebumps, Shadow Zone, and House of Horrors are some of them. It seems the torture of being watched and the sensation of being scared must be enjoyable, at least to readers who return again and again to these books. The books written specifically for teenage readers consistently put females in places where they can be, and are, watched. The female is a target.

THE APPEAL OF TRANSGRESSION

I am speaking of the relatively recent phenomenon of teen horror books, books by writers such as Cusick, Christopher Pike, R.L. Stine, Carol Ellis, A. Bates, Jesse Harris, Joseph Locke, Diane Hoh, and others. In some cases the writer's name is significantly androgynous, and the books themselves pander to a rather familiar stereotype of the passive female/aggressive male that represents a throwback to an earlier era when questions of gender identity were clear and patriarchal. These books clearly derive from the work of such popular authors as Stephen King, Peter Straub, Anne Rice, and perhaps preeminently V.C. Andrews. Andrews' *Flowers in the Attic* (1979) is, and was, a hot read for teenagers. For those of you who haven't read this book, I will briefly fill you in on the plot. Four young children lose their father in a car accident, and they and their mother return to live with the mother's parents in a great country house. The catch is that the grandfather has never forgiven his daughter for marrying the man she married, her cousin, and in order for him to accept his daughter in his home, she must hide her children in the upper rooms of the house. In this act of duplicity she has the compliance of her mother, a stern and witchlike woman who appears to hate the children. To make what is a very long story short, enforced confinement over several years leads to the two older children's commiting incest, and one of the younger children's dying. The grandmother proves to be the witch she seems, and she both physically and emotionally brutalizes the children. The whole thing is nasty in the extreme, full of transgressions and the most unpleasant experiences. The book absolutely gloats over its readers, tantalizing them or her with bursts of violence and promises of perverse behavior.

Flowers in the Attic is an unpleasant read, but young people appear to like it. And publishers are clear on one thing: what the reader likes, the reader will get. If they read it, more will follow. And more books that delight in transgressing the bounds of good taste have followed. In 1993, 8 million copies of Christopher Pike's horror novels for teens and 7.5 million copies of Stine's Fear Street series were in print. And Cosette Kies reports that in 1988, "182 horror novels/anthologies

---

GOOSEBUMPS COME WITH A PRICE

Katherine Kersten, a commentator for National Public Radio's "All Things Considered," writes in the Minneapolis Star Tribune *that she believes R.L. Stine's "shock fiction" harms children by not teaching them compassion.*

Significantly, tragedy—the most frightening of literary genres—is often viewed as the highest human art form. Its first practitioners, the ancient Greeks, believed its power sprang from its ability simultaneously to induce two emotions: fear and pity, or sympatheia—the ability to "feel with" others' suffering. The Greeks viewed suffering as a path to knowledge, both of oneself and of the world. Tragedy, they said, ennobles the human soul by allowing us to "enter into" the sufferings of others, and learn vicariously from their hard-won experience. . . .

Far from encouraging empathy, "Goosebumps" lead children to objectify others, and to enjoy—with morbid fascination—the spectacle of their suffering.

Author Diana West has read 30 "Goosebumps" books. The aim of such "shock fiction," she writes, is to induce a repeated "fight or flight" reaction, a strangely pleasurable sensation in which "stress-induced panic takes over the autonomic nervous system." The result is "reading as glandular activity"—"a crude tool of physical stimulation, wholly devoid of mental,

were published." This, she says, marks "an increase of 90% over 1987." The appeal of such books, Kies goes on to say, is "fun." Whether one likes it or not is, she argues, "all a matter of taste."

FOCUS ON SUPERFICIAL, OUTER TRAPPINGS

They say that you cannot judge a book by its cover, but I'm not so certain this holds true for teen Gothic fiction. Cover after cover of these books shows a single figure, more often than not a female, framed, or what my colleague Mavis Reimer refers to as "targeted," in some way. An ugly knife blade contains the reflection of a blond-haired girl who appears terrified (Stine's *Broken Date*, 1988); a blond-haired young girl stands inside a phone booth, looking out at a threatening shadow visible at the bottom of the picture (Ellis' *My Secret Admirer*, 1989); a young blond girl screams, and we see her framed within the lens of a camera (Pike's *Die Softly*, 1991); a blond-haired young girl lies in bed,

---

emotional or spiritual engagement." In West's view, "Goosebumps" "debas[e] the act of reading, and more important, the reader himself."

What about "Goosebumps" defenders' second argument—that the books are a valuable bridge to quality literature? On the contrary, West writes, the books offer a "preliterate, retarding experience," dulling the very sensibilities children need to become mature readers. Youngsters accustomed to a constant "fix" of sensational incidents are unlikely to thrill to "Where the Red Fern Grows." If they move on to better books, it will be in spite of, not because of, their experience with "Goosebumps." Publishing executives know this. That's why they're churning out millions of even more terrifying books for 9- to 13-year-olds, from R.L. Stine's "Fear Street" series to a host of sordid copycats. . . .

Our children are caught up in the downward spiral of an ever-more-debased popular culture. No harm done, we tell ourselves—we're just letting them "choose for themselves." This consoling thought lets us off the hook, making it easy to abdicate our responsibility as parents and educators. I'm afraid, however, that it is wishful thinking. "Shock fiction" for gradeschoolers comes with a price, and our children will pay it.

Katherine Kersten, "These Books Induce Fear While Driving Out Pity: R.L. Stine's 'Shock Fiction' Comes with a Price," *Minneapolis Star Tribune*, January 29, 1997.

clutching a blanket to her bosom, as she watches a cocky young male materialize in front of her (Stine's *Haunted*, 1990); a young girl is visible in the window of a high school (A. Bates's *Final Exam*, 1990); a young girl with auburn hair stands with her back to us, framed in an iris with flames behind her (Jesse Harris' *The Possession*, 1992); a young auburn-haired girl sits on a bench while an older male figure watches from a window behind her (Stine's *College Weekend*, 1995); a young blond-haired girl, a look of horror on her face, crawls away from rats and toward a looming figure in a hoodlike mask (Cusick's *Silent Stalker*, 1993). The message the reader derives from these covers, and others like them, is that these books offer the secret and socially denied delights of female violation, abuse, and domination.

I refer to the hair of the females depicted not only to suggest the stereotypical nature of the characters depicted in these novels, but also to capture a sense of the novels' collective interest in such outward trappings of appearance. Hair and clothes are nearly always a main feature, sometimes the only feature, of character description. Here's a character named Tyler from Cusick's *The Locker* (1994): "He was wearing an overcoat way too big for him—a long flowing black thing buttoned right down over his black hightops. He was also wearing a black baseball cap, turned around backward." Black serves a dual purpose here: it's the fashionable color (or was in 1994), and it invokes mystery, danger, the brooding Gothic hero, here wearing the badge of every young boy these days, a baseball cap. The narrator of this book is a teenager named Marlee. She goes on to describe Tyler as "really cute," with soft hair. In short, he is "incredibly sexy." Sabrina van Fleet, in Joseph Locke's *Deadly Relations* (Book 2 of Blood and Lace, 1994), is typically beautiful:

> Her skin was so pale, it was nearly translucent, smooth as velvet and without a single blemish. Her eyes were large and a brilliant green with thick, dark lashes that needed no mascara. Her beautiful, heart-shaped face was framed by full, waving, shining blond hair that cascaded over her shoulders and ended just above her full breasts in front and just past her shoulder blades in back.

In R.L. Stine's books we constantly learn what characters wear: "sleeveless blue T-shirt and very Hawaiian-looking baggy trunks," "501 jeans and a pressed button-down, blue workshirt," "tan chinos and a white pullover shirt with the little black Polo pony on the breast"; "a faded Bart Simpson T-shirt over jean cut-offs," "black denim jeans and a red-and-black Aerosmith T-shirt," "a green T-shirt over an orange sleeveless T-shirt over white tennis shorts"; "blue Ralph Lauren sweater over designer jeans," "her big, expensive, fur-lined coat"; "tight, pink bicycle shorts and white midriff tops," "a small gold bikini," "yellow-and-white-striped Giorgio beach bag," "gray sweatpants over a faded Hard Rock Cafe T-shirt." But nothing illustrates the absurdity of this obsession with clothes better than the following passage from Stine's *Beach Party*. You should know that Karen is just about to find her friend Renee murdered in a kitchen:

> Then her [Karen's] eyes wandered down to the floor, and she saw two bare feet, the toes pointing up. Her breath caught in her throat.
>
> She walked closer.
>
> "Renee?"
>
> She peered around the island and saw a girl lying on her back, her mouth open in a frozen O of horror, her eyes wide, unmoving, staring up at the ceiling.
>
> "Renee?"
>
> She was wearing shorty pajamas.
>
> "Renee?"

As you might guess, along with this focus on beauty and fashion, the books present characters who are very much middle-class. The chinos and Giorgio bags are only a slight indication of the books' emphasis on wealth. Characters drive hot and expensive cars: a "navy-blue Mustang convertible," a "1960 Thunderbird" fully restored, "a Ferrari," "a souped-up Trans Am," an "old gray Mustang," "a shiny blue Pontiac Firebird," a "black 1968 Mustang convertible," a BMW, "a brand-new silver Jaguar," and so on. They like expensive and trendy things. Consumerism looks good in the pages of these books.

MODERN "SENSATION" NOVELS

A few of these books rely on a certain intertextuality to give them some semblance of substance. References to some of the more obvious aspects of popular culture turn up: people read Stephen King novels, references to the *Nightmare on Elm Street* films occur, as do references to the *Psycho* movies, *The Wolfman, Ghostbusters, Night of the Living Dead*, and of course *Dracula.* Plots take their form from such recent films as John Carpenter's *Halloween* (Stine's Babysitter books), Adrian Lyne's *Fatal Attraction* (Stine's *The Girlfriend*), Jerry Zucker's *Ghost* (Stine's *Haunted*), Sean S. Cunningham's *Friday the 13th* (Ellis' *Camp Fear*), John Landis' *American Werewolf in London* (Stine's *The Boyfriend*). Characters sometimes have obviously allusive names: Sabrina van Fleet, Lilith Caine, Helen Demeter. Most often, however, names are anonymous, akin to names of soap opera characters: Jenny Fowler, Herb Trasker, Karen Mandell, Katrina Phillips, Rachel Owens, Mark James, Marlee Fleming, Pete Goodwin, William Drewe, and my favorite, Pearce Cronan. Often references to popular culture figures occur: Def Leppard, Tom Cruise, Christie Brinkley, the Ninja Turtles, Matt Dillon, Tom Hanks, and so on. The attempt is to remain familiar and yet to fill the familiar with uncanny happenings. The message is: The familiar world we live in is dangerous, and you'd best get used to it.

The Victorians had books they referred to as "sensation" novels, and these modern Gothic horror books are versions of this kind of book, only marketed directly for the young. As well as stereotypical characters, they offer a racially homogeneous world. Everyone in these books is white, and everyone is acutely conscious of money and status. When characters are "dark," as in *Vampire Twins: A Trilogy,* by Janice Harell (1994), their swarthiness is a mark of their attraction, their mysterious association with things transgressive. The books are interesting in their cynicism. They set out to draw young readers in, using tired formulas that, in effect, make the reading experience predictable and comfortable. Here is titillation without apparent consequences. Here are books that confirm what the young readers already think of the world, and that confirm their interest in fashionable and marketable things. What these books say about their authors' view of young people is sad. The implied readers of these books hate or fear or are distant from their parents; are masses of seething libido; have brutal instincts; are obsessed with fashion and the material objects our consumer society offers; accept the "beauty myth"; use the language of cliché; and accept a view of the world in which violence and victimization are natural.

The villains of these books vary. Sometimes adults, such as an unassuming father (*Babysitter*) or a psychiatrist's receptionist (*Babysitter II*) or a stepparent (*Nightmare Matinee*) are psychopathic. Sometimes female friends are the culprits (*The Immortal, Camp Fear*), but more often than not the stalker or slasher or prowler or murderer is a male member of a group of friends. The motive for murder is usually revenge. In every case, the villain is deranged, and his or her derangement is the result of some psychic scar caused by an unfortunate love affair, a broken family, a humiliation, the mistreatment of a sibling, jealousy. The message, however, remains the same: the prowlers and murderers are among us, members of our own groups and families. The disturbing thing for me about this is the way these books assume that normalcy consists in this condition of threat. Everyone, but mostly young (and blond) girls, is a target for some act of brutality. The world we live in is a world under siege. Rather than decry this situation or depict it as uncivilized, these books suggest that violence is natural and that the human community will always have its crazed members. It's as if Jack the Ripper has become domesticated in some way, normalized, rendered a familiar part of our human community rather than an unacceptable aberration. These books strike me as typical of our postmodern condition; they reflect a world gone crazy, and yet this craziness has somehow become accepted as normal.

In other words, these books reflect a society numbed to the very forces that erode safety and community. Speaking of family, these books depict a world in which no one has a family, no one has security. The individual, especially if that individual is a young, attractive female, finds no security in society; the world we inhabit is dark and ugly. Darkness has truly drawn down; the center has completely fallen apart. The beast has slouched its way here, and walks among and within us. The short rhyme Jenny receives from her friends at the end of *Silent Stalker* says it all:

Don't try to run
Don't try to hide
You won't get far
We're right outside.

Use of Secrecy to Foster Growth

John Daniel Stahl

John Daniel Stahl, a professor of children's literature at Virginia Polytechnic and State University, Blacksburg, believes that the often-used motif of secrecy is a very helpful element in children's books. Secrecy in children's fiction often gives the book's characters a greater sense of their own identity, helps them discover outer truths, and bonds them together in a shared journey. In Stahl's view, the child readers then bring these experiences into their own lives.

The idea of secrecy appeals to adults occasionally, not only to children. What then are the distinctive functions of secrecy for the young reader? It is clear that secrecy and mystery have for young readers the sort of universal appeal that can be exploited by formula fiction. Witness the many books of the Hardy Boys and the Nancy Drew series, as well as many of the books on the mystery shelves of the juvenile department of our libraries. But secrecy is not the province only of cheap mysteries, just as romantic love is not the subject matter only of shallow romances. Secrecy, like initiation or death, is a theme capable of being treated banally or brilliantly. It has the special quality of paradoxically symbolizing not only the author's relation to the reader (reading is an act of entering into a shared consciousness with the writer—a shared "secret"), but also the adult author's relation to the child as character and as reader. The author of a children's book reenacts the mysterious truth that one consciousness can contain another. The child's secret becomes the adult's stated truth.

Excerpted from John Daniel Stahl, "The Imaginative Uses of Secrecy in Children's Literature," in *Triumphs of the Spirit in Children's Literature*, edited by Francelia Butler and Richard Rotert. Copyright © 1986 Francelia Butler. Reprinted with permission from John D. Stahl.

SECRECY CAN LEAD TO SELF-REALIZATION

Secrecy is often the child's method of declaring and developing his or her individuality and independence. Louise Fitzhugh's treatment of a child's secrecy is particularly trenchant in part because her narrative perspective is free of condescension. The narrator in *Harriet the Spy* approximates Harriet's point of view. Harriet's "spying" is really curiosity masked in secrecy; Harriet wants to find out without being found out. Her explorations of various people's lives serve the function of helping her to grow in awareness of the options of adult identity, of what directions she can take in the process of becoming. Secrecy, especially the privacy of her notebooks, is important to her because she needs the opportunity of judging without shaping her responses to the expectations of others, adults and peers. Her notebooks allow her to assess potential adult role models and to criticize cowardice, stupidity, and other faults in her classmates and friends. Fitzhugh emphasizes this function of secrecy by satiric portrayals of adult foibles.

As long as Harriet's thoughts remain secret, she can be honest. The loss of the protection of secrecy leads to a compromise of her integrity. She must pretend to be sorry for what she wrote in order to win back her friends. Though the repudiation of the honesty of her confidences to herself is a necessary compromise for the sake of social growth, through her notebooks Harriet is able to develop her skills as a writer and to explore her perceptions and emotions through her secret dialogue with herself. Many readers of *Harriet the Spy* report starting a journal like Harriet's after reading the book as children, which suggests that the secrecy of Harriet's writing offers children a form of self-realization to emulate.

SECRETS ON THE ROAD TO KNOWLEDGE

"Secret" can be synonymous with knowledge. When Harriet is spying on the bed-loving Mrs. Plumber, she overhears the following conversation:

> "Well," Mrs. Plumber was saying decisively into the telephone, "*I* have discovered the *secret of life.*"
>
> Wow, thought Harriet.
>
> "My dear, it's very simple, you just *take* to your *bed.* You just refuse to leave it for *anything* or *anybody.*"

> Some secret, thought Harriet; that's the dumbest thing I ever heard of.

Harriet is disappointed. She recognizes that this adult's knowledge is clearly affectation or stupidity or both. On the other hand, Mata Hari is a model Harriet is eager to imitate, even when it means learning the—to her—odious skill of dancing. Mata Hari's secret identity and activities guarantee the integrity of her character for Harriet. By testing adults' various kinds of knowledge against her own judgment, Harriet approaches, very imperfectly, to be sure, the Dostoevskian command to love everything and perceive the divine mystery in things.

Through secrecy, children may seek a knowledge of their own which is sometimes forbidden or in danger of being abused by adults. In Frances Hodgson Burnett's *The Secret Garden,* the garden is a place of privacy which needs to be hidden from adults. The garden is directly connected to the awakening of Mary's imagination, and with the development of her own personality:

> The Secret Garden was what Mary called it when she was thinking of it. She liked the name, and she liked still more the feeling that when its beautiful old walls shut her in no one knew where she was. It seemed almost like being shut out of the world in some fairy place. The few books she had read and liked had been fairy-story books, and she had read of secret gardens in some of the stories. Sometimes people went to sleep in them for a hundred years, which she had thought must be rather stupid. She had no intention of going to sleep, and, in fact, she was becoming wider awake every day she passed at Misselthwaite.

In the garden Mary discovers for herself purposeful activity and fulfillment. "If no one found out about the secret garden, she should enjoy herself always," the narrator says, from Mary's perspective. The garden is imaginatively transformed into a magical realm, a place where Colin eventually grows toward healing. Identification with Mary and Colin's pleasure in preserving and enjoying their secret paradise can be a cathartic experience for readers of the book, because the garden is synonymous not only with growth in nature and of personality but with liberation from adult restraints and inner bonds of self-pity and defeat. Burnett achieves a complex rapport with the reader partly because she shows us Mary and Colin truthfully as they appear from an external perspective ("she was a disagreeable child") and sympathetically from within.

THE JOY OF DISCOVERY

Often secrecy in a children's story is not created by the children who are the main characters. In many mystery stories the secret lies in the outside world and presents itself as a puzzle to be solved. Both the inner secrecy (the child's creation) and the outer secrecy (a mystery in the larger world which calls for the child's discovery or quest for discovery) represent ways of ordering experience into meaningful patterns. To give an example of what is here meant by outer secrecy, in the story *The Horse Without a Head* by Paul Berna, a band of children lose their beloved three-wheeled metal horse to mysterious and threatening thieves who apparently place an extremely high value on the battered old toy. The question which the story's events pose and around which the book is structured is, why do the thieves want a seemingly worthless rattle-trap tricycle? The adults are not overly concerned about it all, until it turns out that the horse contains (literally) a key which leads to the solution of an adult mystery. The presence of something unexplained, the effort to find clues about the explanation, and finally the discovery of the desired answer: this sequence in a story is appealing because it is in fact the pattern of such a large part of growing up. Moreover, in recapitulating and symbolizing processes of learning and of the formation of purposeful, goal-oriented activity, the unriddling of mysteries offers a variation of the "principle of hope" (Ernst Bloch's phrase). Like the punishment of evildoers or the successful performance of a trial task in the folktale, the pursuit, discovery, or protection of secrets of literary stories for older children have hermeneutic potential.

SECRECY LEADS TO CHILDHOOD BONDING

Often children who are concerned with secrets will form clubs or gangs at the same time. Private secrets represent the development of an individual identity; shared secrets often denote a shared identity. In *Huckleberry Finn*, Tom Sawyer organizes a band of boys, to be called Tom Sawyer's Gang, which requires an oath and one's name written in blood for admission.

> Everybody was willing. So Tom got out a sheet of paper that he had wrote the oath on and read it. It swore every boy to stick to the band, and never tell any of the secrets; and if any-

body done anything to any boy in the band, whichever boy was ordered to kill that person and his family must do it, and he mustn't eat and mustn't sleep till he had killed them and hacked a cross in their breasts, which was the sign of the band. And nobody that didn't belong to the band could use that mark, and if he did he must be sued; and if he done it again he must be killed. And if anybody that belonged to the band told the secrets, he must have his throat cut, and then have his carcass burnt up and the ashes scattered all around, and his name blotted off the list with blood and never mentioned again by the gang, but have a curse put on it and be forgot, for ever.

Mark Twain has captured with comic accuracy the intense seriousness of children's preoccupation with cementing social ties of their own creation, in fantastic mimicry of romanticized adult models. But the very straightforwardness of Huck's—and Twain's—reporting of these activities itself signals an adult amusement at childish innocence, and invites knowing hilarity without deflating naive identity. The contradiction of thinking of themselves as robbers and murderers (i.e., outlaws) and yet wishing to have recourse to suing in a court of law if their sign is used improperly, of forming an antisociety society, may or may not be evident to any particular child reader.

Mark Twain

The gang is the juvenile replica of adult society, on a smaller scale. Often the gang requires that its activities be clandestine because it seeks to elude adult supervision. Erich Kästner's classic German children's novel *Emil and the Detectives* furnishes an example. Kästner recreates the state of mind of the child who cannot confide certain difficulties to any adult. When Emil wakes up in a train and finds that the money which was pinned inside his coat pocket has been stolen, he is terrified, because he feels he cannot call the police to aid him even though the loss of the money is a very serious matter. Emil has a guilty conscience because he defaced a monument in the park, and expects to be accused and jailed if caught. This is what he thinks:

Now, to top it all, he had to get mixed up with the police, and naturally Officer Jeschke could keep silent no longer but would have to admit officially, "I don't know why, but that schoolboy, Emil Tischbein of Neustadt, doesn't quite please me. First he daubs up noble monuments. And then he allows himself to be robbed of a hundred and forty marks. Perhaps they weren't stolen at all?

"A boy who daubs up monuments will tell lies. I have had experience with that. Probably he has buried the money in the woods or has swallowed it and plans to go to America with it. There's no sense trying to capture the thief, not the slightest. The boy Tischbein himself is the thief. Please, Mr. Chief of Police, arrest him."

Horrible! He could not even confide in the police!

But he can confide in other children. In the metropolis of Berlin, he meets a gang of boys and girls who, once initiated into the difficulties of the situation, organize into a spy ring which eventually tracks down and delivers the thief to justice. All of this happens without adult assistance, and on the sly, of course. The book is the adventurous history of Emil's voyage away from home, alone, into independence from the adult world through the assistance of his peers. The reader's imaginative participation in fictional gangs such as Emil's can be a form of vicarious socialization. The secrecy and self-sufficiency of clandestine children's groups in stories is a form of empowerment of the younger generation. Kästner recognizes and, like Twain, affectionately mocks the tendency of children to mimic adult behavior, for instance in nicknames such as "Professor" and in Emil's cousin Pony Hütchen's ironic formality.

The gang and the secret code are not, of course, desired by all children. In Nina Bawden's *The White Horse Gang*, despite the title, the gang is a loose organization with plenty of internal conflict. Bawden presents the variety of attitudes children at different stages of social development have toward secret organizations. The gang is begun at Rose's suggestion, and neither Sam nor Abe (her friends) are enthusiastic.

They both looked at Sam. "All right," he said. "We'll call it the White Horse Gang. And we got to have a secret sign."

Giggling, Rose placed her left forefinger against the side of her nose. Sam suggested that they should use the other hand at the same time, and pull at the lobe of the right ear, but Abe said they didn't want to make it too obvious.

"And we'll sign our names backwards," Rose said. She looked

blissfully happy, so happy that neither boy could bring himself to protest that this was a childish device. They practised with a pencil stub on an old bus ticket Sam had in his pocket. Esor and Mas and Eba. "That's lovely," Rose sighed. "'Course, we ought really to sign in *blood.*"

"Blood's for kids," Sam said. He had once got a septic finger from pricking and extracting blood for this purpose. "What we want more is a *reason.*"

In its portrayal of the conflicts that separate and distress the members of the White Horse Gang, Nina Bawden's book is more psychologically realistic than Erich Kästner's smooth-working, effective Robin-Hood-style gang; Kästner's book is in this respect closer to fantasy. But whether in realistic or in mythic guise, the fantasy is of a kind very appealing to children; it has a great deal of resonance in children's experiences. The secret club or gang appeals to dream-wishes for group identity, and represents an early recognition of the truth that there is strength in numbers. The secret organization provides readers with fantasy versions of substitute families and of social roles among one's peers which are not determined or monitored by adults.

SELF-IDENTITY THROUGH SECRECY

Secrecy is a means for fictional characters to create a meaningful sense of self, frequently in productive, not necessarily hostile, opposition to grown-ups or rivals. One value of such themes lies in children's being encouraged to imagine similar sources of self-awareness in their own lives. In Astrid Lindgren's *Bill Bergson Lives Dangerously* some of the appeals of secret signs, secret languages, and secret organizations are made more explicit than in many books for children, surely one of the reasons for the popularity of Lindgren's work. The book opens with the war of the Red Roses against the White Roses, and it becomes clear that the war and the mystery surrounding it, especially the secrecy about the totemic object called the Great Mumbo, are ways of introducing purpose and entertainment into random, dull experience: "Bill grinned contentedly. The War of the Roses, which with short interruptions had been raging for several years, was nothing one voluntarily denied oneself. It provided excitement and gave real purpose to the summer vacation, which otherwise might have been rather monotonous." The Whites (with whom the story is primarily concerned) have a secret language, which involves doubling each consonant and placing an "o" in between. The Whites can flaunt their identity with their secret language: "There was no surer way of annoying the Reds. Long and in vain they had tried to decipher this remarkable jargon which the Whites spoke with the greatest facility, chattering at such insane speed that to the uninitiated it sounded like perfect babel." When the Reds capture and interrogate Anders, the leader of the Whites, he does not reveal any secrets under "torture."

Lindgren's narrative perspective does not disguise adult awareness of children's maintenance of secrets. In fact, it acknowledges secrecy as the child's way of creating self-identity; but the open, indulgent attitude of the adult narrator defuses potential conflicts between generations. Eva-Lotta, a member of the Whites, meets her mother in the market place. When asked where she is going, Eva-Lotta says, "That I must not tell. . . . I'm on a secret mission. Terribly secret mission!" Despite Eva-Lotta's refusal to tell, the exchange between mother and daughter is affectionate and amusing:

> Mrs. Lisander smiled at Eva-Lotta.
>
> "I love you," she said.
>
> Eva-Lotta nodded approvingly at this indisputable statement and continued on her way across the square, leaving a trail of cherry stones behind her.

Her mother's acceptance of Eva-Lotta's right to have secrets is a liberating, loving attitude. That the secret mission represents the development of an independent personality is suggested by Mrs. Lisander's concerned thoughts about her daughter: "How thin the girl looked, how small and defenceless somehow! It wasn't very long since that youngster had been eating biscuit porridge, and now she was tearing about on 'secret errands'—was that all right, or ought she to take better care of her?"

But Eva-Lotta's experiences are narrated also from a perspective that implies the child's need and ability to face danger on her own. For a while, a secret box, containing mysterious documents, is the object of an entertaining struggle between the Reds and the Whites. But secrecy only comes into full play in a dangerous situation when Eva-Lotta is alone with a murderer in an abandoned house. The murderer has every reason to kill her: she holds the key to knowledge of his guilt. When Anders and Bill arrive in this frightening situation, she communicates with them through secret signs: with the danger sign, then with a song in secret code that tells the boys that the man is a murderer. The boys respond with another secret sign (pinching the lobes of their ears) which means that they have picked up the information. Here, quite explicitly, children have to protect themselves from harm from the adult world through the code they have created. Secrecy is necessary for self-preservation, just as in *Nobody's Family Is Going to Change* the "Children's Army" has to conceal its existence from adults in order to function effectively as a children's rights advocacy organization.

Lindgren, like many other of the best of children's authors, is able to convey the comic incongruities of childhood experiences without diminishing their significance. In the final chapter of *Bill Bergson Lives Dangerously,* after the murderer has been captured, the Whites teach the Reds their secret language. Bill explains why: "We can't have it on our consciences, letting the Reds walk about in such dreadful ignorance. They'll be absolutely done for if they ever get mixed up with a murderer". Though that statement may strike an adult reader as comic, murder is not minimized in the book. Eva-Lotta's reaction to finding the body of the murderer's victim is a state of shock that realistically lasts several days. Despite the implausibilities of the plot, the theme of secrecy is treated with a seriousness that does justice to its importance as a means of achieving identity and as a defense against the danger of harm by powerful adversaries.

THE AUTHORS' SYMPATHY FOR CHILDHOOD SECRETS

Secrecy in children's literature, in a variety of forms, emphasizes the ambivalent consciousness of the adult author writing for children. The adult, having once been a child, has access to memories of childhood in the form of internalized experience—the alter ego that always remains a child within us. But the adult writer also has a mature and sophisticated consciousness that analyzes the child's experience and the child's placement in many contexts of family, society, psychological and moral development, inheritance, and environment. The triumph of the spirit in children's literature that reflects children's preoccupation with secrecy lies in skilled authors' ability to combine the dual perspectives of childhood and adulthood in an instructive tension. At the root of this illuminating tension lies respect for the development of the child's personal and social identity. Sympathetically conceived works of fiction invite imaginative participation in the experiences of fictional characters who create and discover secrets. Like fairy tales, stories about secrets and secrecy have imaginative connections with children's psychological and social development which go beyond the literary qualities of particular stories. But the artistry of works such as those discussed here connects the private world of the child's imagination with the reality of experience and with the realm of all great literature.

Underestimating the Importance of the Everyday-Life Story

Deborah Stevenson

Children's literature scholar Deborah Stevenson, argues that novels about a child's everyday life have long been underestimated and underappreciated by critics and academics. These stories allow children to identify with the characters' lives and experiences, and thereby help them to grow. Using author Beverly Cleary's popular Ramona series as an example, Stevenson points out why these books continue to be so popular with children, and why they give children a greater sense of self.

Stories of everyday life, of family, and of school exist for children of all ages, and such stories provide the bulk of contemporary American children's literature for readers aged eight to twelve. They are popular with children and often cherished by adult practitioners and critics, yet they are frequently lost in the shadow of books more stimulating to adult readers and scholars. Taking as synecdoche and as example Beverly Cleary's extremely successful books about Ramona, I examine the light this undervaluation casts upon children's literature's history, practices, and criticism, and the ways in which this undervaluation ironically mirrors the treatment children's literature itself has frequently received.

Children's literature is not, of course, monolithic, nor are children's literature authorities, a term I employ to include practitioners—librarians, teachers, and parents—who work with children, as well as critics who write upon or teach the subject. There is no choric voice speaking one overriding viewpoint, and there have been adults who have championed this kind of children's fiction or considered it worthy of analysis. These adults, however, are exceptions to the field's

Excerpted from Deborah Stevenson, "Ramona the Underestimated: The Everyday-Life Story in Children's Literature," in *Reflections of Change: Children's Literature Since 1945*, edited by Sandra L. Beckett. Reprinted with permission from Greenwood Publishing Group, Inc., Westport, CT.

general disinclination to consider the everyday-life story not just a worthwhile but also a creditable literature. . . .

JUDGING A BOOK BY ITS COVER

At the heart of this question of undervaluation is the question of value itself. What makes a book singularly meritorious? Originality or familiarity? Entertainment or education? Understandability or challenge? What kinds of books make a genre meritorious? What kinds of books will make the world take this literature seriously? The topics of the Newbery medalists in the past few years include death, morality, and race relations, all subjects that adults respect as worthy matter, all subjects that demonstrate how serious and substantial children's literature can be. Even if Louis Sachar's *Marvin Redpost: Why Pick on Me?* had been considered the best children's book of 1994, children's literature authorities would not have awarded their ultimate prize to a book about nose-picking—what would the neighbors say?

One manifestation of children's literature's attempts at self-justification is the valorization of books that most strongly resemble adult books. Although everyday-life stories feature prominently on children's-choice award lists and circulate to a feverish degree, the adult-judged awards and the adult critical attention tend to go to books of a more traditionally "weighty" nature: those that treat, in [social theorist Mike] Featherstone's terms, heroic life rather than everyday life. Critics find their material in dramatic fantasies, controversial problem novels, and pivotal coming-of-age sagas, shying away from the challenge of books where the family does not break down and where no great tragedy occurs—from, in short, books whose merits may uniquely depend upon their audience.

Francelia Butler suggests that English departments sneer at children's books as "the literature with the washable covers", the response of children's literature authorities has generally been outraged denial and a claim that young-adult fiction is nearly as good as adult fiction, rather than an invitation to such sneerers to discover the merits of washable covers. Even critics writing on Beverly Cleary seem more at ease discussing her novel for older readers, *Dear Mr. Henshaw* (1983), than they do the Ramona books: Geraldine DeLuca applauds *Dear Mr. Henshaw* for handling "many matters that the bulk of her work avoids," and Pat Pflieger, in her monograph on Cleary, states that *Dear Mr. Henshaw* "deserves deep analysis on its own," which presumably the remainder of Cleary's works do not. Children's literature authorities often seem to feel that their literature needs to grow up to become adult literature, just as its readers need to grow up to become adults; praise is often meted out according to how close a book comes to that adult ideal.

Attempts to demonstrate that children's literature can tackle serious subjects often produce books that seem to be watered-down versions of adult literature: there are quite a few dystopias, I would argue, superior to Lois Lowry's *The Giver* (1993), many of them understandable to children of the same reading level. The fact that such a book is in many ways like an adult book seems often to blind adult readers to the fact that those adult books are, by most traditional literary standards, better books. *The Giver* is, however, a more exciting book for children's literature critics than are most everyday-life stories. American children's literature offers a few dystopias, but they are almost exclusively post-apocalyptic tales written for a young-adult audience, so Lowry's book deals with issues of morality in a way that seems innovative within the genre. The appearance of innovation fades, unfortunately, when one views the book in terms of both adult and children's literatures; it resembles an adult book only so long as no one actually compares it with adult literature. Even this illusory and ephemeral resemblance, however, gives the book and, correspondingly, the genre of children's literature a glamour that the workaday everyday-life story never can.

EVERYDAY HEROES

The classic everyday-life heroine, Ramona first appeared as a supporting, albeit never minor, character in Beverly Cleary's books about Henry Huggins; she pushed her way to a title role in *Beezus and Ramona* (1955) and then took her rightful place in the spotlight in six books: *Ramona the Pest* (1968), *Ramona the Brave* (1975), *Ramona and Her Father* (1977), *Ramona and Her Mother* (1978), *Ramona Quimby, Age 8* (1981), and *Ramona Forever* (1984). Initially a wayward toddler, she has triumphantly become a big sister and a third-grader by the final book, but she is essentially the same impulsive person dealing with the same difficult demands of getting through daily child life throughout the series. She has been a favorite of young readers from the very beginning and continues to be even today, over a decade after her last appearance. Many of the characteristics that have made these books successful, however—their humor, their quotidian subject matter, their proclivity toward serial appearances—and even that very popularity inhibit their serious critical consideration.

Like many everyday-life stories, the Ramona books rely extensively on humor. Humor is in some ways a double-edged sword: books that are particularly humorous may win more attention for this feat but will rarely garner the serious attention given to books of a more sober tone. Light comedy is a traditionally undervalued field in virtually every art: when it is done well, it looks too easy, and humor in children's fiction offers delicate directorial challenges to which many authors fail to rise. American awards committees rarely select a comedy for the ultimate prizes; to state that a funny story is the ultimate in children's literature is, it seems to be feared, to suggest that children's literature is as light and insignificant as it has often been painted.

Nor does the subject matter of these books help stave off skeptical charges of insignificance—there is no human death or life-threatening illness, no global crisis, no painful realizations of racism or sexism in the chronicles of Ramona; these are not stories of great heroism. While there is conflict in Cleary's books, that conflict is not the point of the books in the way it is in other children's fictions. Everyday-life stories describe interaction with peers at school, struggles with sibling rivalry at home, or anticipation of a holiday; they end usually for temporal reasons (e.g., summer is over) rather than reasons of climax or resolution. It often seems that each volume simply chronicles the struggle to make it to the next book.

Everyday-life stories not only demonstrate but also depend upon predictability: friends fall out; teachers teach, or upset, or both. In such fictions for older audiences, protagonists as young as fifth and sixth grade start wondering about members of the opposite sex. Perry Nodelman notes that "most children's books are 'simple,' undetailed, and consequently, so similar to each other that their generic similarities and their evocations of archetypes are breathtakingly obvious." Such "simple" books can begin to seem homogeneous to the adult reader, and series of everyday-life stories featuring the same protagonist begin to blend together.

Such a lack of episodic differentiation is, to a certain extent, the point. Were a new Ramona book to appear, one would not ask (nor would one with books about most other classic everyday-life stories) what the book is "about," because it is about Ramona. They are all about Ramona. What overtly differs in each book is the season, or perhaps how her father's efforts at finding a job he likes have been rewarded, or if she likes her new teacher, but these differences do not necessarily distinguish the events in one book from those in another. What is important is Ramona's overall growth and reflection, not the events that cause them. Each of Cleary's books shows Ramona at a different stage of Ramonaness than she was in the previous book, as she, like the reader, matures, but she is still Ramona, and therein lies the point of continuing to read her exploits. With their focus on recurrent visits with the same character, everyday-life stories as exemplified by the Ramona books are devoted to the sheer literary pleasure found, as Wayne Booth says, in his book so titled, in "the company we keep."

As Jane Tompkins points out, these characteristics of predictability, circumscription of pleasure, and apparent literary safety are not those that critics are accustomed to venerating. As child readers relish the return of their favorites and appreciate the books all the more for the familiarity of the hero or heroine, adults grow less interested in what appears to be more of the same, no matter how well crafted the same is. To practitioners and critics, who read a great many everyday-life stories, the subject matter can begin to seem clichéd regardless of the merit of the writing or the memorableness of the main character. Where child readers value familiarity, adult authorities distrust it; to hold up as meritorious a book that is conspicuously lacking in originality, obviously resembling the author's other works about the same character, is to suggest that this book is good in spite of—or, more challengingly, because of—its flouting of the traditional merit of originality.

STARTING FROM A DISADVANTAGE

Some of the most significant feminist criticism since the mid-1970s has challenged the devaluation of literature popular with and written for a devalued class; much of this criticism is meaningful for the discussion of children's literature as well. Jane Tompkins points out that "the *popularity* of novels by women has been held against them almost as much as their preoccupation with 'trivial' feminine concerns." If one replaces "by women" and "feminine" with "for children" and "childish," that statement applies to contemporary children's everyday-life stories much as it did to nineteenth-century domestic fiction. I would go on to contend that, despite the strong presence of women in nearly every aspect of the production of children's literature, Tompkins' charge that criticism equates "popularity with debasement, . . . domesticity with triviality, and all of these, implicitly, with womanly inferiority" still and often applies to academic criticism of children's literature.

Like feminist criticism, "children's literature criticism has had to come out of a corner fighting"; like much feminist criticism, children's literature criticism often displays a strongly defensive tone, repeatedly explaining, in the face of anticipated opposition, the worth of studying these books and frequently commenting, sometimes bitterly, about the critical underestimation of such texts. Such defensiveness is not necessarily misplaced in either kind of criticism, both kinds of scholarship have been denigrated as trivial, dismissed as an unimportant women's concern, and ignored. Since both women and children operate from positions of diminished power, it would be inappropriate to overlook this effect on their literatures. It is nonetheless notable that, in criticism of both kinds of literature, the criticism's perception that it is itself struggling against opposition infuses the scholarship to such a degree and for such a duration.

Children's literature, especially in America, is a female-dominated genre, and the everyday-life story is historically a strongly female literature, [as critic Cornelia Meigs notes] "written always by women for the reading of girls." Yet everyday-life stories are rarely valorized by the feminine discipline that judges them; behind this devaluation of the daily is a struggle against the perceived femininity of children's literature. While the female shaping of children's literature sometimes works to the genre's advantage, the counterreaction to that female predominance, that determination to fight the categorization of children's literature criticism as "nursery" criticism, contributes to keeping these "feminine" books from receiving the ultimate accolades. Practitioners and critics of both sexes underplay the role of these domestic fictions in children's literature in order to prove the genre's seriousness. These books evoke too much affection both from adult practitioners and from child readers to disappear from libraries and bookshelves because of this undervaluation, but these fictions are, as a result of this struggle for recognition, casualties of critical regard.

This constant struggle for justification, this "generic self-image," as Zohar Shavit terms it, permeates much critical writing on children's literature and influences children's literature authorities' recognition of individual titles and of types of literature. The field's newness to the academy and its uncertainty encourage it to adopt conservative views of literary merit and critical purpose, views that adult literary criticism has seriously challenged for some time. As children's literature attempts to establish and justify itself according to those views, it treats the everyday-life story with the same affectionate condescension with which adult literary criticism has often viewed children's literature.

Nicholas Tucker describes children's literature as "backward-looking"; there is a widespread, albeit not unanimous, opinion that children's literature's very merit lies in its resistance to new forms, that it is, as Isaac Bashevis Singer called it, "a last refuge from a literature gone berserk and ready for suicide." The literature tends to replicate the tastes of the past, the childhood of the adult rather than the experience of the contemporary child; the criticism, in its attempt to justify the literature and itself, tends similarly to cling to venerable methods of scholarship, which offer an illusion of solidity. While other literary genres are contemplating dismantling their canons, children's literature, in volumes such as the Touchstones series, or Charles Frey and John Griffith's *The Literary Heritage of Childhood: An Appraisal of Children's Classics in the Western Tradition* (1987), is attempting to build one. Karin Lesnik-Oberstein points out that even Peter Hunt's important criticism incorporates a subtle and apparently unquestioning reliance on adult literary theories, such as canonization, literary influence, and reader theory, whose validity has been seriously challenged. Aidan Chambers' classic essay "Three Fallacies About Children's Books" opines that many children's literature critics like finding in children's literature the kind of solid, old-fashioned story they appreciate, and that they intend to ensure the continued existence of such literature; I would suggest that many such critics employ a "solid, old-fashioned criticism" that over-looks some of the greatest merits of the genre.

PASSED UP BY AWARDS AND PUBLISHERS

Using awards to judge a genre can be misleading, but the choice of recipients for major distinction, such as the New-bery Medal, is still revealing. Awards are by their very nature designed to reward important books. They are also tacit statements about the genres from which the awardees come, demonstrating not only which books are important within a particular genre but also that the genre, by extension, is itself important. The series of judgments of importance that make up the Newbery list offer an interesting insight into what has appeared significant to representatives of the children's lit-erature community over the years. The last everyday-life story to win even an honor citation was *Ramona Quimby, Age 8*, in 1982, and these fictions did not feature prominently before that (the last time a classic everyday-life story won the Newbery Medal itself was in 1952).

Most recent medal winners combine a social challenge of some kind with a straightforward, almost old-fashioned telling of a tale; in short, the books have been very literarily conservative, in terms of literature as a whole, and have the-matically acknowledged a contemporary concern either overtly or metaphorically. And while committee members are limited to judging the books published in one particular year, it is nonetheless significant that Beverly Cleary won her Newbery Medal not for her everyday-life stories about Ramona but for her serious novel about dealing with di-vorce; Lois Lowry not for her everyday-life stories about Anastasia but for her serious novels about the Danish resis-tance and about the soul-destroying immorality of a repres-sive system; Phyllis Reynolds Naylor not for her everyday-life stories about Alice but for her serious novel about a boy who earns his maturation by championing an abused dog.

Random House has an easy-reader imprint, Stepping Stone Books, that includes several everyday-life stories. That series title is revealing. Adults tend to consider everyday-life stories as stepping stones, paths to something else that is the real destination. These are the books we give children to read until they are capable of reading "real" books. Yet all chil-dren's literature is, essentially, a stepping stone on the way to somewhere else; the more children's literature authorities suggest or imply that the stepping stoneness of everyday-life stories makes them insignificant, the more such critics implicitly devalue the entire genre of children's literature.

The very existence of children's literature depends on an acceptance of the mutability of evaluative criteria; if literature that is superlative for one is superlative for all, then children's literature, with its acknowledgment of the effect of experiential, biological, and conceptual differences on reading, should not exist. Yet critics often seem to hold all books within the genre to a single standard of literary merit, occasionally conceding the usefulness of successful books for younger readers but clearly considering them inferior as literature. This tendency results in a fundamentally flawed approach to notions of merit, since to take this standard to its end would suggest that the book of excellence can exist only for the reader of excellence, that excellence is a knowable and fixed trait in readership and literature, and that excellence in literature is more important than significance in reading experience. One cannot consider the relative merits of *Ramona the Pest* and, say, *Great Expectations* or even *The Chocolate War* without considering their respective readerships.

Jane Tompkins regrets "a long tradition of academic parochialism" that depends on "a series of cultural contrasts: light 'feminine' novels vs. tough-minded intellectual treatises; domestic 'chattiness' vs. serious thinking"; these theories of dichotomy exist in children's literature, too, and have resulted in criticism that fails to consider that very parochialism and its cost. Children's literature will never become the adult literature it wishes to emulate; if it does, it will cease to be. Its strengths lie, as Jane Tompkins suggests, in continuing to push beyond this parochialism and in appreciating its own productions as they walk their peculiar and intriguing tightrope between adult desires and children's responses. Let us learn from the error of adult literary criticism and recognize the power of literature that we might otherwise dismiss as cute, or insignificant, or trivial, or safe. Everyday-life stories are children's literature in microcosm; without valuing them, children's literature cannot value itself.

Exploring Death Through Children's Books

Francelia Butler

Francelia Butler, an English professor and founder of the Children's Literature division of the Modern Language Association, demonstrates that death has been a persistant theme in children's literature. First appearing in early folk tales, fairy tales, and children's rhymes, death eventually became a popular topic in children's fiction and many writers have not been shy in addressing it. Butler points out that often death is portrayed to children not only as an eventuality that should simply be accepted, but as a state that is not necessarily final. She believes this is intended to give children hope and a greater understanding not only of death, but of life.

C.S. Lewis, whose "Narnia" fantasies for children are one expression of his religious philosophy, observed that "a children's story is the best art form for something you have to say." Like a parable—or sometimes, an epitaph—the limpid simplicity of the form makes it easier to see into the depths, even of death.

Once upon a time, children and adults shared the same literature and together understood what there was to be understood about death. That time was from the beginning of literature up until the end of the seventeenth century, when a separation began to take place between the literature of adults and that of children. From then on, the treatment of death became part of a larger problem—the commercial and psychological exploitation of children through a special literature aimed at them alone.

Indications are that the separation might have begun with the "Warnings to Apprentices," published by commercial interests in the seventeenth century. These bear a striking resemblance to the warnings to little children, the "deathbed confessions" of children who disobeyed moral "laws" and reformed too late. Numerous books of these confessions were published in England and America by the Puritan merchant class in the late seventeenth and eighteenth centuries. These deathbed confessions and other dire warnings to children were continued in the hundreds of Sunday School tracts which grew out of the Sunday School movement begun by Robert Raikes. Raikes, a wealthy shipowner, acknowledged that he began the Sunday Schools to keep working children from depredations on Sundays. These tracts distorted goodness itself by getting children to do the right things for the wrong reasons. Raikes' family ties with John Newbery, who is considered to be the "father" of children's literature, could be one indication that the establishment of children's literature as a separate field had an economic basis.

EARLY LITERATURE IMPLIED LIFE AFTER DEATH

Before the seventeenth century, children learned about death in literature shared with adults. They heard Bible stories, fables, legends, ballads, folk tales, or folk plays or read them themselves. Death could be seen in proper perspective because in this literature all the convictions, fears, and hopes of people about many things were gathered up and transmitted.

For the most part, this literature encouraged hopes for life after death in some form. Stith Thompson's *Motif-Index of Folk Literature* abounds with references to restoration to life, either by magical reassemblage of the body's dispersed members, or by administration of the water of life, or by medicines, or in various other ways. Men may come back as women or women as men. People may become children, dwarves, monsters, princes or princesses, stars or angels or gods. They can return to earth as fish, horses' heads, donkeys, cows, bulls, oxen, calves, buffalo, swine, wild boar, goats, cats, dogs, lions, wolves, rabbits, foxes, deer, seals, bears, hyenas, jackals, elephants, monkeys, rats, otters, ducks, owls, hawks, eagles, swallows, cuckoos, doves, pigeons, ravens, quails, partridges, herons, cranes, geese, peacocks, parrots, snakes, lizards, crocodiles, tortoises, or frogs. Or they may come back as bees, butterflies, fleas, weevils, bedbugs, salmon, goldfish, sharks, whales, leeches, scorpions, crabs. Again, they may turn into trees, roses, lilies, lotus, grass, straw, herbs, bramble-bushes, tobacco plants, peanut plants, eggplants, musical instruments, dishes, fountains, balls, wind, stones, salt, smoke, rainbows, minerals, meteors, hills, flour vats, hoes, hoe-handles, mussels, or currants. Or, after a variety of transformations, they may return to their original human form. In any case, the possibility of coming back as an eggplant or a fish, for instance, should sharpen one's interest in ecology. The hopeful note in folk literature is that people *do* tend to come back.

In North American Indian tales, as Jaime de Angulo's beautiful crystallization suggests, life and death are closely related, are at times interchangeable states. However, in some American Indian tales, people stay dead:

> Nearly all North American Indian tribes offer some explanation of the origin of death. The most widespread tale is that of an early controversy between two characters, either animal or human. One character wants people to die and be revived, the other wants death to be permanent. The second character wins the controversy. Often, a little later, a close relative of his, such as the son, dies and the parent wishes the decision reversed. His opponent reminds him, however, that he himself has already decided the matter.

A similar matter-of-fact acceptance of death is occasionally found in European folktales, as in Grimm's story, "The Death of Partlet," a story left out of most Grimm collections. As the story ends in Grimm,

> Chanticleer was left alone with his dead Partlet. He dug her a grave and laid her in it, and raised a mound over it, and there he sat and mourned her till he died too. So they were all dead.

Children themselves seem to begin with this same simple acceptance of death. In the still very active oral tradition, in the skip-rope rhymes jumped by children from the age of six on, and chanted much earlier, children treat death quite matter-of-factly:

> Little Miss Pink
> Dressed in blue
> Died last night
> At quarter past two
> Before she died
> She told me this:
> When I jump rope
> I always—miss.

By writing the American Field Service, which solicited the rhymes from foreign lycées, and also through writing foreign embassies in Washington, I have made a collection of these rhymes. One contributed by the New Zealand Embassy goes:

> There was an old woman and her name was Pat,
> And when she died, she died like *that,*
> They put her in a coffin,
> And she fell through the bottom,
> Just like *that.*

Restoration to life is the general rule in children's play, however. "Bang bang, you're dead!" is only a figure of speech.

One of the many stories of restoration to life in the Grimm collection is the famous "Juniper Tree" story. In this story, a little boy who has been murdered by his jealous stepmother and made into a tasty stew for his father, comes back as a bird to reward his loving father and little sister and to drop a millstone on his stepmother's head. As a bird, he sings about what has happened to him:

> My mother made a stew of me,
> My father ate it all.
> My little sister wept to see
> Marlene, my sister small,
> Then gathered my bones in her silken shawl,
> And laid them under the Juniper tree.
>   Sing, hey! What a beautiful bird am I.

After the stepmother's death, the bird becomes a little boy again and rejoins his family. When the stepmother dies, however, she dies for good; for the wicked, death often provides irreversible retribution. It brings death or rigidity, turns one to a statue or a stone.

Various Approaches to the Topic

Andrew Lang's Fairy Books of various colors date back to the nineteenth century, but they have always been loved by children and furnish an excellent cross section of the folk tales from all parts of the world. In these volumes, there are at least a dozen stories of special interest which relate to death. In *The Orange Fairy Book,* there is a story from India entitled, "The King Who Would See Paradise." The theme here seems to be that though Paradise may be one's lot eventually, one should not hasten the process, but prepare for the end by performing as perfectly as possible one's duties while on earth. *The Pink Fairy Book* contains a Spanish story, "The Water of Life," in which a sister, wiser and more courageous than her brothers, fetches the magic water and restores not only her brothers, but "a great company of youths and girls" who have been put under an evil spell and turned to stones.

The Red Fairy Book contains a Rumanian story which attempts to explain death. People feel impelled to follow a
mysterious Voice and are never seen again. When the source
of the Voice is finally located, it turns out to be nothing but a
vast plain. After that, people don't bother to follow the Voice
anymore, but simply die at home. *The Crimson Fairy Book*
has a more cheerful story—one of a prince who seeks immortality and gets it. In this Hungarian tale, the Queen of the
Immortals and Death himself fight over a youth. The Queen
wins. *The Yellow Fairy Book* has a North American Indian
story which combines elements similar to those in the story
of Pygmalion, and the Orpheus and Eurydice legend. When
an Indian's wife dies, he makes a wooden doll just like her
and dresses it in her clothes. The doll comes to life, but the
husband is under a prohibition not to touch her until they
have returned to their own village. He can't wait and she becomes a doll again. In *The Violet Fairy Book* are two Swahili
stories in which animals, in one a gazelle and in the other, a
snake, sacrifice their lives so that human beings may live.
The Lilac Fairy Book contains another Swahili tale—this one
about a clever monkey who professes to keep his heart in a
safe place at home, when he travels. This idea of an external
heart or soul is not infrequent in folk tales. It is a means of
safeguarding one's immortality by keeping it stashed away—
not putting all one's organs in one's body, so to speak. The
other tale has to do with a fish who achieves immortality. A
tree arises from his buried bones. This tale is unusual because, even in Christ's use of them in the New Testament,
fish are expendable . . . one of the innocuous animals that
ends up as food for people and the act of killing fish is blotted out, some way.

Though there are a variety of approaches to the subject of
death in these stories, all in all the approach is not morbid.
Generally in folk tales, the magic potion which conquers
death is love. One sees this in the German folk tale, "Briar
Rose," or essentially the same, the French story, "The Sleeping Beauty." As G.K. Chesterton observes in his essay, "The
Ethics of Elfland,"

> There is the terrible allegory of "The Sleeping Beauty," which
> tells how the human creature was blessed with all birthday
> gifts, yet cursed with death; and how death also may perhaps
> be softened to a sleep.

Nor does this death-conquering love have to be sexual.

Stravinsky's ballet, "The Firebird," has acquainted many westerners with the Russian folk tale of "Prince Ivan, the Firebird, and the Gray Wolf." Murdered by his evil brothers, "Prince Ivan lay dead on that spot exactly thirty days; then the gray wolf came upon him and knew him by his odor:

> Then the gray wolf sprinkled Prince Ivan with the water of death, and his body grew together; he sprinkled him with the water of life, and Prince Ivan stood up and said: "Ah, I have slept very long!"

In the legends enjoyed by children, the hero has power, even over death. In the Norse legend of "Thor's Unlucky Journey," Thor is challenged to a wrestling match with Utgard-Loki's old nurse, Eli, who, unbeknownst to him, is Old Age or Death: "It was a marvel," said Utgard-Loki, "That you withstood so long and bent only one knee."

In [William] Caxton's version of *Le Morte d'Arthur,* from which many children's versions, including Lanier's *Boy's King Arthur,* stem, Arthur commands Sir Bedivere to throw Arthur's sword, Excalibur, into the water. Bedivere throws the sword far out, and sees an arm and hand reach above the water, take the sword, brandish it three times and vanish. Then Sir Bedivere takes the dying King on his back and carries him to the waterside. Here a barge is drawn up, with many fair ladies in it, all of them wearing black hoods. At the King's command, Bedivere puts him on the barge, and the barge moves away:

> Than sir Bedwere cryed and seyde,
> "A, my lorde Arthur, what shall becom of me, now ye go frome me and leve my here alone amonge myne enemyes?"
>
> "Comforte thyselff," seyde the kynge, "and do as well as thou mayste, for in me ys no truste for to truste in. For I muste into the vale of Avylyon to hele me of my grevous wounde. And if thou here nevermore of me, pray for my soule!"

Roland, in all versions of the Charlemagne cycle, blows a note of defiance in the face of death. Here is a version for children:

> Count Roland's mouth was filled with blood. His brain had burst from his temples. He blew his horn in pain and anguish. Charles heard it, and so did his Frenchmen. Said the King: "That bugle carries far!"
>
> Duke Naimes replied:
> "'Tis that a hero blows the blast!"

When The Cid dies, in a current children's version of this Spanish legend, the embalmed body of The Cid leads a victorious charge against the enemy:

> It was The Cid himself who led the charge, mounted upon Babieca, his sword Tizone gleaming by his side! This was too much for Yusuf and too much for his army. The legends were all true! This Cid was really a demon from hell! Here he was, raised from the dead, charging relentlessly down on them!

Best known of the many retellings of the Robin Hood story for children is probably that of Howard Pyle. Here, too, Robin Hood seems to be in control, even of his death:

> His old strength seemed to come back to him, and, drawing the bowstring to his ear, he sped the arrow out of the open casement. As the shaft flew, his hand sank slowly with the bow till it lay across his knees, and his body likewise sank back again into Little John's loving arms; but something had sped from that body, even as the winged arrow sped from the bow.

MAGIC AND DRAMA

Universally, in folk plays, which are shared both by children and adults, there is an element of wonder, of fantasy, in the ritual death so often portrayed and inevitably followed by restoration to an even more vigorous life. Fertility symbol or whatever it may be, this death and resurrection is accepted both by audience and the players—and these plays continue in some sections of the world. In the mummers' play of St. George, for instance, St. George may kill the Turkish Knight (there are many versions of the play), but then the Doctor invariably enters with a special medicine:

> It will bring the dead to life again.
> A drop on his head, a drop on his heart.
> Rise up, bold fellow, and take thy part.

Also, in the Punch and Judy shows, which in their present form probably date to the eighteenth century but which may date back to the fertility rituals in Greek and Roman mimes, Punch literally triumphs over Death, or the Devil.

One finds in folk drama the concept of life as a journey towards death, a journey in which children and adults move on together, the morality, "Everyman," being the notable example of this theme. In such plays, the traveler is guided by the various tenets of his faith, his deeds being the mileposts of his progress.

The strong dramatic element in life as a journey is found in many folk tales, including those among Indians in the Middle American area, where "The underlying theme is that the soul on its way to the afterworld is confronted by dangers and difficulties which must be overcome." Some of these, such as going between clashing rocks or over a body of water, are reminiscent of the Greek or Roman epics. The idea of life as a journey toward death peeps through most notably, perhaps, in children's literature in the nineteenth century in Louisa May Alcott's *Little Women,* where Meg, Jo, Amy, and Beth (who is about to die) go on a pilgrimage from cellar to attic—a more realistic journey than that in [John] Bunyan [author of *Pilgrim's Progress*]—and later receive small copies of *Pilgrim's Progress,* in colored bindings, under their pillows as Christmas gifts. [Hans Christian] Andersen's "Little Mermaid" also must make a journey from sea to land and undergo much suffering—must die that others may love—before she wins an immortal soul. Nor is it enough purgation for Tom, the chimney sweep in Charles Kingsley's *The Water-Babies,* to be brutally beaten by his Master and maltreated by everyone in contact with him. Even after he drowns and becomes a water-baby, he still must undergo a long Jungian journey and spiritual purification—must help someone he doesn't like (his old Master, Grimes).

BEING CANDID ABOUT DEATH

Besides folk tales and folk drama, another form of literature for children which has ancient roots is the fable. Though there is currently no satisfying popular edition, there are several bowdlerized editions of *Aesop* published by various companies every year. We know that Caxton's translation of *Aesop* was read both by children and adults, and John Locke repeatedly recommends *Aesop* for children. Here the relation of all aspects of human experience is quite complete—including sexual experience—complete enough to make spicy reading for *Playboy.* (But this shouldn't bother us if we have seen the rhymes chanted today by children themselves and recorded in the seventy-fifth volume of the *Journal of American Folklore.*) Here is one of the "death" fables from Caxton's *Aesop:*

> Many one ben whiche haue grete worship and glorye/ But noo prudence/ ne noo wysedom they haue in them whereof Esope reherceth suche a fable/ Of a wulf which found a dede mans hede/ the whiche he torned vp so doune with his foote/ And sayd/ Ha a how fayr hast thow be and playsaunt/ And now thow hast in the neyther wytte/ ne beaute/ yet thow arte withoute voys and without ony thought/ And therefore men ought not only to behold the beaute and fayrenesse of the body/ but only the goodnes of the courage/ For somtyme men

gyuen glorye and worship to some/ whiche haue not de-
seruyd to haue hit/.

Alas, poor Shakespeare and Milton, who were limited to
reading like this, instead of having the benefit of such contemporary emptiness as *Michael Is Brave* (a frightened little
boy learns courage by showing a little girl how to go down a
slide), or any of the other hundreds of commercial books
(we shan't call them literature) by one-message tacticians in
the Puritan tradition, who—no matter how they may try to
sugarcoat the message—talk down to children. Sir Roger
L'Estrange's *Aesop*, which came out two years after Locke
had recommended *Aesop* for children's reading, states
specifically in the preface that it is designed for children and
has nothing unsuitable for childish ears. Yet it is just as explicit about all areas of human experience as is Caxton's.

A more recent book for little children, *Life and Death*, by
Herbert Zim and Sonia Bleeker, also is explicit, but the focus
is on factual and scientific information:

> Long ago people had the idea that death was like a long sleep.
> Children think so too. This belief is far from the truth. A
> sleeping animal or a sleeping person is alive. He breathes, his
> heart beats, he moves, dreams, and will react to a touch or a
> poke. Someone who is dead does none of these things.

Later on, the book candidly tells the child:

> After burial a body, which is composed of nearly three-quarters
> water, soon changes. The soft tissues break down and disap-
> pear first. Within a year only bones are left.

Such man-in-the-white-coat treatment lacks warmth and
beauty and is certainly not sufficient for initiating children
to the subject of death. In many commercial books for children now, there is a paucity of imagination, a lack of philosophical reflection, something missing. Their spiritual ni-
hilism is in itself a moral message in the Puritan tradition.
Truth, these books imply, can only be determined by scientific testing. Zim and Bleeker stand for no philosophical
truth. Instead, they indifferently display various beliefs on a
kind of religious lazy Susan: "There is no way," they say, "to
know if these beliefs are true or not. They are beyond our
power to test or experiment."

The inadequacy of such books as literature for children
on the subject of death is commented on by Sheila R. Cole in
an article which appeared in *The New York Times Book Review*. Miss Cole summarizes her observations as follows:

All of these stories were written with a didactic purpose: to give a child a way of looking at death and living with the knowledge of it. All of them try to diffuse the finality and fearfulness by presenting death as just another natural process. But to most adults in our culture, death is more than just another natural process. It is an occasion surrounded with mystery and deep emotions. Presenting it to a child as just another change we go through is less than candid. Adults often present a prettier reality to children than actually exists. But to give easy answers to a child's questions about death is to deny reality and to diminish both life and death and, ultimately, to turn our children from our counsel.

—"For Young Readers: Introducing Death" (September 26, 1971), p. 12.

HONEST EMOTION

In the nineteenth century, the neurotic writers of the classics for children expressed at least some honest emotion. Freud wasn't around yet, and they felt safe in exploding their problems—homosexuality or other—into childish rhymes and fantasies. Filled with guilt, these writers were constantly aware of death. In [Edward] Lear's limericks, supposedly light rhymes designed both for children and adults, death is a leading topic, as Alison White has pointed out. There was, for example, "The Old Man of Cape Horn,/ Who wished he had never been born/ So he sat on a chair till he died of dispair." Professor White surmises (as Elizabeth Sewell suggested earlier in *The Field of Nonsense*) that "in his limericks Lear, like all of us, is trying to get used to death, to dull its sting."

Perhaps Professor White's explanation will also serve for the grim death jokes which critics have noticed in *Alice in Wonderland*:

> "Well!" thought Alice to herself, "after such a fall as this, I shall think nothing of tumbling down stairs! How brave they'll all think me at home! Why, I wouldn't say anything about it, even if I fell off the top of the house!" (which was very likely true.)

Children themselves have many grimly comic—"mini-dramas"—about death:

> Look, look, mama!
> What is that mess
> That looks like strawberry jam?
> Hush, hush, my child!
> It is papa
> Run over by a tram.

Ushy gushy was a worm
A little worm was he
He crawled upon the railroad track
The train he didn't see.
Ushy gushy!

Besides Lear and [Lewis] Carroll, two other writers of the nineteenth century who seem to have given vent to their emotional problems in their writings for children were J.M. Barrie and Oscar Wilde. In *Fifty Works of English and American Literature We Could Do Without,* J.M. Barrie is accused of making *Peter Pan* the vehicle for his triple theme of incest, castration, and homosexuality. Barrie is also criticized for his treatment of death in the play. Say the authors:

It's not enough, however, for Barrie to betray children. He betrays art. He does it brilliantly. That superb piece of engineering (the engineering, however, of an instrument of torture), the scene where Peter Pan appeals to the children in the audience to keep Tinker Bell alive by clapping to signal their belief in fairies is a metaphor of artistic creation itself. . . . Peter Pan blackmails the children, cancels the willingness of the suspension of disbelief, and disrupts the convention on which all art depends when he threatens to hold the children morally responsible for Tinker Bell's death unless by a real act—an act done in the auditorium, not on the stage—they assert their literal belief in what they know to be an artistic fiction.

In Barrie's defense, one can say that he is asking the children to do what many fairy tales do—that is keeping the protagonists alive through an act of love.

All five of Oscar Wilde's famous fairy tales for children have death as their theme. In the best known of the tales both "The Selfish Giant" and the little boy he loves die. The little boy is identified as Jesus. "The Happy Prince" (a statue) persuades a swallow to pluck the ruby from the Prince's sword, the sapphires from the Prince's eyes, and the gold leaf from his body and give it to the poor in the city. By the time these acts of charity have been accomplished, it is too late for the swallow to fly South for the winter.

"I am glad that you are going to Egypt at last, little Swallow," said the Prince, "you have stayed too long here but you must kiss me on the lips, for I love you."

"It is not to Egypt that I am going," said the Swallow. "I am going to the House of Death. Death is the brother of Sleep, is he not?"

And he kissed the happy Prince on the lips, and fell down dead at his feet.

> At that moment a curious crack sounded inside the statue, as
> if something had broken. The fact is that the leaden heart had
> snapped right in two.

The saddest of Wilde's stories is "The Nightingale and the
Rose." A little nightingale sees a student weeping for a red
rose. The student's girl has said she would dance with him
if he brought her such a rose. The nightingale seeks a rose
for the youth, and is told by a tree that the only way such a
rose can be obtained is for the nightingale to build it out of
music and stain it with her own heart's blood. The nightingale must sing to the tree all night, with her breast against a
thorn (an old English belief, by the way, as to how nightin-
gales sing). The thorn must pierce her heart, and her life-
blood must flow into the tree. "Death is a great price to pay
for a red rose," cried the nightingale:

> So the Nightingale pressed closer against the thorn, and the
> thorn touched her heart, and a fierce pang of pain shot
> through her. Bitter, bitter was the pain, and wilder and wilder
> grew her song, for she sang of the Love that is perfected by
> Death, of the Love that dies not in the tomb. . . .

> "Look, look!" cried the Tree, "the rose is finished now;" but
> the Nightingale made no answer, for she was lying dead in
> the long grass with the thorn in her heart.

The student finds the rose outside his window and presents
it to the girl, but she spurns it as the Chamberlain's nephew,
meanwhile, has sent her some jewels. Disgusted, the student
throws the rose down in the street, and a cartwheel runs
over it.

> "What a silly thing Love is," said the Student as he walked
> away. "It is not half as useful as Logic, for it does not prove
> anything, and it is always telling one of things that are not go-
> ing to happen, and making one believe things that are not
> true. In fact, it is quite unpractical, and, as in this age to be
> practical is everything, I shall go back to Philosophy and
> study Metaphysics."

> So he returned to his room and pulled out a great dusty book,
> and began to read.

Cynically, the student throws away the emotional and picks
up the scientific.

DEATH AS A PUNISHMENT

Even though these stories sound like dreams recounted on a
psychoanalyst's couch, they do have the ring of honesty,
which can be tested by comparison with the Puritan educa-

tional propaganda for children, in which death is a punishment for sin. Closely related in theme to the "Warnings to Apprentices" of the late seventeenth century, numerous deathbed confessions of young children stemmed from James Janeway's *A Token for Children: Being an Exact Account of the Conversions, Holy and Exemplary Lives, and Joyful Deaths of Several Young Children* (1671). These continued to be printed in small American towns during the eighteenth and nineteenth centuries. The Connecticut Historical Society in Hartford has a number of these little books and several are listed in the A.S.W. Rosenbach catalog of *Early American Children's Books.* Their reflection is seen in *The New England Primer,* many editions of which contained these verses:

> Tho' I am young yet I may die,
> And hasten to eternity:
> There is a dreadful fiery hell,
> Where wicked ones must always dwell.

As if the poor American Indian children had not suffered enough, even they were subjected to these deathbed confessions, and in 1835, *Triumphant Deaths of Pious Children* was translated into Choctaw by Missionaries of the American Board of Commissions for Foreign Missions. What is more, these deathbed confessions of children merged imperceptibly with the nineteenth century Sunday School literature, so that we have, for instance, *An Authentic Account of the Conversion, Experience, and Happy Deaths of Ten Boys,* designed for Sunday Schools, and published in New Haven (1820).

Here is a quotation from one of the early nineteenth century Sunday School booklets published for children by the American Tract Society in New York. Since I have not located it elsewhere, I am quoting from a copy in my own collection:

> Why should you say, 'tis yet too soon
>   To seek for heaven, and think of death?
> The flower will fade before 'tis noon,
>   And you this day may lose your breath.

> Then 'twill for ever be in vain
>   To cry for pardon and for grace;
> To wish you had your time again,
>   Or hope to see the Savior's face.

This gloomy literature allied itself easily with the sentimental attitude toward death in the mid-nineteenth century, famous examples being Hans Christian Andersen's stories of "The Little Fir Tree," "The Steadfast Tin Soldier," and "The

Little Match Girl." Then there is the death of Little Eva in Harriet Beecher Stowe's *Uncle Tom's Cabin*. Often, in the sentimental literature, the child does not die for his own sins but for the adultery of adults—his parents—and the trend here is found in adult literature as well, as in Mrs. Wood's *East Lynne*. Always quick to penetrate hypocrisy, Mark Twain in *Tom Sawyer* has the boys, supposedly dead, return to witness their own funeral and to hear themselves eulogized as saints by those who hated their humanity while they were alive in the town:

> First one and then another pair of eyes followed the minister's, and then almost with one impulse the congregation rose and stared while the three dead boys came marching up the aisle, Tom in the lead, Joe next, and Huck, a ruin of drooping rags, sneaking sheepishly in the rear! They had been hid in the unused gallery listening to their own funeral sermon!
> (*Tom Sawyer*, Chapter 17)

Thus, the boys have the double satisfaction of getting back at their parents or parent-figures and, at the same time, of witnessing their own "death" and resurrection.

In our own time, one of the best known instances of death as a punishment for a mistake (or at least, death as closely associated with the mistake or sin) is that of the death of the good Thorin in Tolkien's *Hobbit*. Thorin's greed for the great jewel, the Arkenstone, to which he feels rightly entitled, leads to a fight. Though the quarrel is resolved, Thorin dies and the Arkenstone is buried with him. Thus Thorin (and possibly the readers) learns the worthlessness of material things.

A KIND OF IMMORTALITY

One of the most notable treatments of death in children's literature is by E.B. White in *Charlotte's Web*. White makes an interesting blend of fantasy and realism: when the little spider dies, she lives on through her 500 offspring, through the memory of the extraordinary web-writing she did above the stable door, and through the love of her friend, the pig Wilbur. White is to be commended for facing a subject which most writers for children now avoid—though not all children are content, I find, with the prospect of a selective immortality for those with children or extraordinary ideas or (short-lived) friends. Still, such lines as these have beauty, pathos, and, above all, sincerity:

> Nobody, of the hundreds of people that had visited the Fair, knew that a grey spider had played the most important part of

all. No one was with her when she died.
>*(Charlotte's Web,* Chapter 21)

For the fullest treatment of death in children's literature, we must return to the nineteenth century, to the fantasies of George MacDonald, most notably to *At the Back of the North Wind* and *The Golden Key.* George MacDonald (1824–1905) was a Scottish preacher influenced by Paracelsus, Boehme, Swedenborg, Blake, Wordsworth, Novalis, and negatively, by Calvinism. He in turn exerted an influence on Lewis Carroll, Ruskin, C.S. Lewis, Charles Williams, and J.R.R. Tolkien. Since most of his family died of tuberculosis, including four of his own children, MacDonald (who also suffered from the disease) was understandably preoccupied with the subject of death.

To some extent, his writings combine the various attitudes toward death, for they embody a simple acceptance of death and fear of death and the conviction finally that death is "more life." He believed that child-like qualities are eternal; he believed that all life goes through a mystic evolution, each step of which on the way up is attended with sacrifice; and one is tempted to conclude from his fantasies that he believed that through love, faith, and the imagination one can create one's own Paradise and make it real.

But one must be careful not to be too explicit about meanings in MacDonald's fantasies about death. What they say is all the more effective because it is not pinned down. One must simply make the leap of faith into his stories. As W.H. Auden says in his Afterword to MacDonald's *Golden Key,*

> But to hunt for symbols in a fairy tale is absolutely fatal. In the Golden Key, for example, any attempt to "interpret" the Grandmother or the air-fish or the Old Man of the Sea is futile: they mean what they are. The way, the only way, to read a fairy tale is the same as that prescribed for Tangle at one stage of her journey.

And Auden quotes the following passage from the story:

> Then the Old Man of the Earth stooped over the floor of the cave, raised a huge stone from it, and left it leaning. It disclosed a great hole that went plumb-down.

> "That is the way," he said.

> "But there are no stairs."

> "You must throw yourself in. There is no other way."

My own feeling is that the vagueness of MacDonald's fantasies is not a deliberate artistic accomplishment but an accident induced by an imperfect fusing of his own thought with his reading in Paracelsus, Boehme, and Novalis.

I think he wrote the fantasies because he needed deeply to believe them, but that ultimately he did not altogether trust them. The despondent silence of his last five years might serve as evidence. But I also believe that he wrought better than he knew, and that the blurred picture he produced was intuitively good, for it frees the imagination of the reader.

In St. Exupéry's *The Little Prince*, which Martin Heidegger is said to have regarded as "one of the great existentialist books of the century," the Little Prince deliberately goes out to meet the snake which he knows will return him to the earth, cause his death:

> There was nothing there but a flash of yellow close to his ankle. He remained motionless for an instant. He did not cry out. He fell as gently as a tree falls. There was not even any sound, because of the sand.

The supreme act of giving is his death. It washes over him like a great wave and returns him to the cycle of nature. His courageous act of faith is not unlike the leap demanded of Tangle in *The Golden Key*. And it bears a striking symbolic resemblance to the leap demanded of all human beings in a strange Vietnamese folktale, "The Well of Immortality." In this folktale, the God Nuoc comes to earth and stations himself at the bottom of a deep well. He calls up that those who have the faith to leap down to him will become immortal. But people hesitate. Instead of leaping, they dip their fingers and toes and the tops of their heads in the water. And this is all the immortality they get—their nails and hair continue to grow after death.

After the disturbing reaches of the fantasies of MacDonald or of St. Exupéry, it is rather a relief to turn to the old-fashioned Christian Platonism of C.S. Lewis' Narnia series, concluded in the seventh book *The Last Battle:*

> "The Eagle is right," said the Lord Digory. "Listen, Peter. When Aslan said you could never go back to Narnia, he meant the Narnia you were thinking of. But that was not the real Narnia. That had a beginning and an end. It was only a shadow or copy of the real Narnia, which has always been here and always will be here: just as our world, England and all, is only a shadow or copy of something in Aslan's real world. You need not mourn over Narnia, Lucy. All of the old Narnia that mattered, all of the dear creatures, have been drawn into the real Narnia through the Door. And of course it is different; as dif-

ferent as a real thing is from a shadow or as waking life is from a dream." His voice stirred everyone like a trumpet as he spoke these words: but when he added under his breath "It's all in Plato, all in Plato: bless me, what *do* they teach them at these schools!" the older ones laughed. It was so exactly like the sort of thing they had heard him say long ago in that other world where his beard was grey instead of golden.

How is it best to introduce a child through literature to the idea of death? Folk literature, the amalgam of human experience, and some of the great fantasies seem to indicate that the honest and warm human approach is best—not talking down to the child because of his age, for death knows all ages, but simply telling him what we know, what we don't know, what we fear, and what we hope. We find this approach in folk literature, which, as Tolkien might put it, is the very bones of the stock of human experience in which there is frequently a close and friendly relationship between life and death. The predominant attitude toward death is simple acceptance, combined very often with a belief that death is not final, that it is to be accepted, even actively embraced with the sure knowledge that through love, a resurrection will occur.

CHAPTER 4

Controversy in Children's Literature

Challenging, Censoring, and Banning "Inappropriate" Books

Maria B. Salvadore

Maria B. Salvadore, a children's services librarian in Washington, D.C., realizes that children's books are a particularly easy target for censorship since they contain such a wide array of sensitive topics for educators, parents or librarians to seize upon. In the quest to protect children from potential harm, many books are challenged on political, moral, or religious grounds. The past two decades have witnessed a rise in the number of books banned from schools and libraries.

It can be said with great assurance that everything is bound to offend someone, with controversy the usual result. Children's books most often become controversial because of political, moral, or religious convictions; portrayals of women, ethnic minorities, racial differences and stereotypes, sex and sexuality, or violence; and, of course, language considered profane or otherwise offensive.

Controversies over many children's books have little to do with their literary merit and much more to do with adults' views of what is appropriate for children. Books can be potent forces and are perceived as more permanent—hence, more powerful—than the fleeting images seen on television or movie screens. Because of this perception, children's books may stir sharper controversy than do other media. Ideologies, perceptions, and language change in a changing society, and thoughtful reassessment of children's reading can be healthy if the literature and its readers are respected.

RELIGIOUSLY OFFENSIVE AND POLITICALLY INCORRECT

Political and religious controversy can arise over a seemingly marginal detail in a work or over the work's central premise or theme. William Steig's picture book *Sylvester and the Magic Pebble* (1969) clashed with the politically charged climate of the 1960s and was harshly criticized for its portrayal of the police. Sylvester, a young donkey, happens upon a magic pebble, is transformed into a rock, and is thus separated from his loving parents. Frantic, Sylvester's parents (also donkeys) seek help from the police, depicted as concerned pink pigs in blue uniforms. Where readers today recognize a satisfying story, cleverly told and illustrated and happily resolved, readers in the 1960s were sometimes offended by a depiction that seemed to evoke the then common derogatory epithet for police officers.

Also viewed as political commentary rather than literature were *The Lorax* (1971), a fantastic, rhyming, environmental cautionary tale by Dr. Seuss, and *Eli's Songs* (1991), by Monte Killingsworth, a novel of a twelve-year-old boy's growing self-awareness, set in Oregon, where a threat to an old-growth forest parallels the dramatic changes in the boy's life. Both books were charged with bashing the timber industry and were declared inappropriate for children in some communities of rural California.

In 1993 Laurence Yep's *Dragonwings* (1975) occasioned a court case in Pennsylvania. This moving story of a Chinese immigrant and his son who dream of building a biplane in the San Francisco of the early 1900s was accused of advocating Taoism, reincarnation, and secular humanism, religious convictions to which the complainant was opposed.

SOCIALLY UNACCEPTABLE BEHAVIOR

Perceived challenges to mainstream social mores arouse controversy as well. The picture books *Heather Has Two Mommies* (1991), by Leslea Newman, and *Daddy's Roommate* (1991), by Michael Willhoite, consciously attempt to help children understand a potential source of anxiety for being "different" and suggest the viability of nontraditional families in their presentation of children living with gay parents. Only marginally effective in terms of plot, character development, and illustration, the mere presence of a lesbian couple and of a gay father and his lover in books for children has caused a swirling controversy. Those who argue in favor of these books contend that they depict the kind of family in which many children live. Opponents object to the books' nontraditional moral and religious values and alternative lifestyles.

A more subtle social challenge—in a more artistically effective work—can similarly arouse the ire of some adults. In *Harriet the Spy* (1964), by Louise Fitzhugh, Harriet's spy notebook, filled with her brutally honest observations, falls into her friends' hands, and under the stress of discovery, the eleven-year-old's behavior deteriorates rapidly. Harriet's busy, socialite parents cannot cope and send her to a psychologist; Old Golly, Harriet's eccentric former nanny, writes to suggest that Harriet learn to tell small lies to prevent hurting others' feelings. Harriet does, and her friendships are restored. Is Fitzhugh advocating, in this humorous, well-crafted novel, that children should lie or that well-meaning parents should seek professional help for their errant children? Not likely, but where children empathize and even identify with Harriet, laughing at her exploits, some adults are offended by Fitzhugh's portrayal of adults and this "rude" child.

CULTURAL AUTHENTICITY

Heightened sensitivity to our society's multiethnic make-up has led to close scrutiny of the portrayal of minorities in contemporary books for children as well as reexamination of earlier works. Books from earlier eras, when reexamined, may receive harsh criticism from contemporary readers who impose on them their anachronistic perspectives. Consider the seemingly endless discussion about the perceived racism in Mark Twain's *Adventures of Huckleberry Finn* (1884) or the sexism ascribed to Wendy's passive role in J.M. Barrie's *Peter Pan* (1911).

Contemporary works can elicit similar concern. In *Jump Ship to Freedom* (1981), by James Lincoln Collier and Christopher Collier, protagonist Daniel Arabus, a young slave in post-Revolutionary War America, must cope with a dishonest master and with his yearning for freedom. His trials cause him to question his own capabilities, but through his response to them, both Daniel and the reader, by novel's end, recognize his intelligence and worth. The authors' use of the hurtful language prevalent in the eighteenth century and their depiction of the character's self-doubt have caused many concerned adults to question the book's impact on contemporary African American children and, since the Colliers are not African Americans, the authenticity of the point of view.

Cultural authenticity has also been at the center of a minor controversy over Jennifer Armstrong's *Chin Yu Min and the Ginger Cat* (1993), a picture book describing how a haughty Chinese woman learns humility through friendship with a cat. Although the angular figures in the stylized artwork have been criticized as perpetuating a harmful, offensive stereotype, other critics contend that the strong form and line of the illustrations represent not stereotypes but a distinctive style.

PROTECTING CHILDREN FROM VIOLENT TEXTS

Many adults believe that children must be protected from the portrayal of violence and things unsettling. Maurice Sendak's visual interpretation of two Nursery Rhymes in *We Are All in the Dumps With Jack and Guy* (1993) is intentionally unsettling, portraying a dark world in which thin, ill-clad children live in cardboard structures and are pursued by human-sized rats and where Jack considers knocking a "little boy with one black eye" on the head. Children may see such scenes on city streets and in television news programs, but many adults question whether they are appropriate in a children's book.

Controversy around Sendak's interpretations of a child's world is not new. Not only did Max's sassiness to his mother disturb adults who read *Where the Wild Things Are* (1963), but so did the Wild Things themselves. They were and, to some adults, still are too frightening, too unsettling, too potentially violent for young children.

Nowhere is violence in children's literature more apparent than in folktales. A troll is "crushed to bits, body and bones," in the "Three Billy Goats Gruff"; two out of three pigs become a wolf's snack in pre-Disney versions of the "Three Little Pigs"; the nasty sisters' toes and heels are mutilated as they attempt to wear the golden slipper in "Aschenputtel," the Grimm version of "Cinderella." Probably no body of literature has created the number of recurring controversies that folktales have, though no body of literature has had a greater or more lasting influence. The Grimm tale "Hansel and Gretel," despite wide distribution in picture-book editions and in story collections, remains controversial for its portrayal of stepmothers, child abuse, and violence.

Folktales have their defenders. They are satisfying stories with clear conflict, straightforward characterization, and appropriate resolutions, and they allow children—according to psychologist Bruno Bettelheim—"access to deeper meaning, and that which is meaningful to [the child] at his stage of development." Folk and fairy tales, says Bettelheim, "stimulate [the child's] imagination; help him to develop his intellect and to clarify his emotions; be attuned to his anxieties and aspirations . . . while at the same time suggest solutions."

THE ALA'S TOP TEN LIST

USA Today *ranks the ten most often challenged books from 1990 to December 1, 1999, according to the American Library Association. In that time period a total of 5,600 challenges were reported.*

1. Daddy's Roommate, Michael Willhoite (96)
2. Scary Stories series, Alvin Schwartz (92)
3. I Know Why the Caged Bird Sings, Maya Angelou (60)
4. The Adventures of Huckleberry Finn, Mark Twain (53)
5. The Chocolate War, Robert Cormier (48)
6. Bridge to Terabithia, Katherine Paterson (45)
7. Of Mice and Men, John Steinbeck (45)
8. Forever, Judy Blume (40)
9. Heather Has Two Mommies, Leslea Newman (36)
10. The Catcher in the Rye, J.D. Salinger (32)

Olivia Barker, "Popularity of 'Potter' Stirs Cauldron of Dissent: Books' Foes Cite Rights of Parents, Free Speech," *USA Today*, December 28, 1999.

Mother Goose rhymes, too, despite their perennial popularity as satisfying, brief stories with playful, easy-to-understand rhythm and language have been criticized as being too violent. All violence or potentially offensive references have been written out of *The New Adventures of Mother Goose: Gentle Rhymes for Happy Times* (1993), by Bruce Lansky. In this sanitized version, "three blind mice" don't chase the farmer's wife and get their tails cut off "with a carving knife"; rather, "three kind mice" run "after the farmer's wife," take "out some cheese/ and they cut her a slice." The satisfying mini-adventure offered by Mother Goose has been replaced by a saccharine revision, in accordance with some adults' view that only "happy times" are appropriate for children.

UPROAR OVER SEX AND PROFANITY

Perhaps the most provocative issue in children's books is sex and sexuality. Examples of books that have violated this societal taboo include Maurice Sendak's *In the Night Kitchen* (1970), the now classic (and ever-popular) story of Mickey's fantastic nighttime adventure, with its depiction of a frontally nude Mickey, and Judy Blume's young adult novel of first love and sexuality, *Forever. . .* (1975).

"Dirty" or profane language can create similar controversy. The title character in Katherine Paterson's novel *The Great Gilly Hopkins* (1978) is an unhappy child, moved from one foster home to another, always believing that her mother will return. Gilly's language reflects her misery and her determination to drive people away from her. Though entirely in keeping with her character, it is Gilly's occasional use of offensive language, not her isolation or unhappiness, that has frequently stirred controversy. A novel, Paterson wrote, "cannot . . . set examples, it must reflect life as it is. And if the writer tells her story truly, then readers may find in her novel something of value for their lives." The lasting value of this novel extends far beyond the words in Gilly's vocabulary.

Adult offense at the use of "dirty" words in books for children is sometimes so strong that it leads to censorship. In one example, an elementary school headmaster abruptly removed Lois Lowry's humorous, contemporary novel *Anastasia Krupnik* (1979) from his school when the book, which had been available to his students for more than a month, unhappily fell open in his sight to a page that contained an offensive word. His prohibition, of course, merely assured for months thereafter the constant use of the public library's copy. In another incident, the book was first removed and then returned to a school library—with the offending words whited out. Eleven-year-old Anastasia used a "dirty" word to express frustration with her parents and with the impending arrival of a new child. Her language, as well as that used by Paterson's Gilly, is appropriate within the context of the book's character, plot, and theme; only when seen in isolation does it become controversial.

Literature provides pleasure and understanding. It can inform, inspire, interpret, amuse, arouse, and more. It cannot, as C.S. Lewis once wrote, protect a child from "the knowledge that he is born into a world of death, violence,

wounds, adventure, heroism and cowardice, good and evil."
But literature can help the child to clarify that world. As long
as there are children and books there will be controversy.
Perhaps in the end, controversy simply indicates that adults
care about the books children read because they believe in
the power of literature.

Stereotypical Female Characters in Popular Children's Books

Marjorie N. Allen

Marjorie N. Allen, a children's book author and reviewer, believes that the messages young girls receive in books affect the way they feel about themselves and influence their understanding of a woman's place in the world. If adolescents are presented with unrealistic or outdated fictional characters as role models, it can negatively affect their self-esteem. Allen considers titles from the past and present which illustrate this issue, and shows that fortunately, this problem is abating.

Adolescence is not the first time girls become aware of gender roles, of course. Many books for young readers, some published decades ago and still popular, introduce girls to traditional, often outdated, expectations. Children's books before the 1970s presented childhood as a time of innocence. Gender roles were clearly set forth, as in Inez Hogan's *The Upside Down Book* (1955), which presented "A Story for Little Boys" in pages of blue and "A Story for Little Girls" all in pink, with a teddy bear for the boy and a doll for the girl. Activities for the boy included climbing trees, sliding down hills, and dealing with accidental falls, while the girl takes her doll to the park and tells her to be careful, gets a Popsicle and warns the doll not to get it on her dress, and at the end of the day makes sure all her toys are put away. A child reading this book learns that boys are expected to be active and girls are expected to be passive. This assumption still exists, with parents of toddlers taking pride in the fact that their little boy is drawn to guns and trucks, while their little girl loves playing house. Whether this behavior is inborn or learned is still being debated.

EARLY IMAGES

In Carolyn Haywood's popular *"B" Is for Betsy* (1939), a story about five-year-old Betsy's kindergarten experiences, almost every stereotype defining gender is present. Betsy depends on Father to resolve any problem she faces; the teachers in Betsy's school are all females; the traffic monitor is a police*man;* all of the animals in the book are male, except for one dog, who has to be a female because she has puppies—male puppies. Pink is the prevalent color for girls: a pink-and-white tea set on a bed of pink cotton, pink roses and pink candles on Betsy's friend Ellen's birthday cake, even pink ice cream. At a costume party, Betsy is dressed in pink, while her friend Billy carries a whip and wears a toy revolver in his belt. In this book, grand-mothers bake cookies and mothers are housewives.

In pre-1970s children's books, the transition from child-hood to adolescence was rarely discussed. Happy endings were the rule, and subjects such as divorce, sex, drugs, and death were avoided. Haywood's books reflect the social cli-mate of the 1930s and 1940s, when children were protected from adult concerns. The popularity of *"B" Is for Betsy* has continued, regardless of its stereotypes, because there were and still are few chapter books directed at five-year-olds. The larger print and simple language appeals to early readers.

When Maud Hart Lovelace wrote *Betsy-Tacy* (1940), she avoided stereotypes altogether and even managed to make a reference to the death of one character's baby sister. This is a story of two five-year-old girls who are independent and imaginative and develop a close friendship, solving their own problems instead of seeking adult intervention.

According to feminist theorist Judy Mann, imagination helps many girls through various forms of adversity as they grow up. One common fantasy of girlhood is to be de-scended from royal blood, which, when revealed, will allow a little girl to reign supreme "over her father and other grown men." Frances Hodgson Burnett's *A Little Princess* (1905) is an example of this type of fantasy, although in the case of young Sara Crewe, she has always been a princess to her father. When he is reported dead, she loses her status and is abused by the schoolmistress and jealous classmates. Her status is eventually restored through the efforts of adult males, but Sara, through it all, retains her self-confidence and belief in herself and shares these qualities with the other girls at the school.

As a topic of class discussion in schools, the story can be seen as a reflection of the social class system in 19th-century England. Sara exhibits strength of character and the ability to empathize with others, traits that ultimately endear her to her peers, and good storytelling in this popular book eclipses any tendency toward didacticism.

NANCY DREW BREAKS THE STEREOTYPE

While *A Little Princess* takes place in England, where class distinction prevails, the indomitable and independent Nancy Drew is the American version of royalty, a superstar who rises above the ordinary and becomes the personification of a dream for many little girls. Although she made her debut in 1930, she exhibits attributes that many young girls still admire today: She is clever, brave, and determined, yet stylish and graceful. She shows none of the ambiguities that typically beset girls in early adolescence. As author Karen Plunkett-Powell says of the Nancy Drew series as originally conceived, "[Nancy Drew] has star quality." She is the "Barbie of the written word, the Shirley Temple of the teen set, the Dorothy of detection, complete with her own Oz-like hometown of River Heights and her own dog named Togo."

In early versions of the series, though Nancy may look down on those she considers inferior, she always solves her cases and never lets boy-girl feelings interfere with her goals. She works well alone or with others. When Edward Stratemeyer created her, and Mildred Wirt Benson (the first "Carolyn Keene") established her personality in *The Secret of the Old Clock* (1930), Nancy was already beyond adolescence and wasn't concerned about what others thought of her. Her enthusiasm was infectious as she set out to solve every case that came her way.

Unfortunately, when a new version of the series, called the "Nancy Drew Files," was created in the 1980s, the qualities that originally made Nancy a role model were submerged in an effort to make her one of the in-crowd, where she is more concerned with romance than mystery. These later books focus on plot rather than character, and Nancy seems to have a lesser role.

Nancy Drew, American princess personified, has always been the most popular female sleuth in the series genre, but she wasn't the only one to make an appearance in the 1930s.

In 1932, the first Judy Bolton mystery (*The Haunted Attic*) was published, and that popular series continued until 1967. The 38 books in the 35-year series recently were reissued in facsimile editions and perhaps because all were conceived and written by the same author—Rachel Irene Beebe under the pseudonym Margaret Sutton—the character of Judy Bolton is more realistic than that of Nancy Drew. Judy is bright and compassionate, but she isn't perfect. She cares what people think of her. "'I'm not afraid of anything,' [Judy] declare[s], 'unless—unless it's being unpopular. I want people to like me.'" She also moves from one neighborhood to another and has to adjust to a new environment, while Nancy's hometown, River Heights, offers stability. For a time, Judy's worst fears come true when she is shunned by her schoolmates. Nancy Drew represents an idealized "James Bond" image, while Judy Bolton can be considered the forerunner to the characters in Judy Blume's realistic, issue-related books of the 1970s. At the time the Judy Bolton series was written, no other books for girls addressed the concerns of adolescence.

JUDY BLUME AND THE TRIALS OF ADOLESCENCE

With the introduction of Margaret in Judy Blume's *Are You There, God? It's Me, Margaret* (1970), puberty became the pop subject of the day. Margaret Simon, at age 11, hasn't started her period yet and wants desperately to get her first bra. Her character speaks directly to generations of girls with these concerns, and Margaret's story is their story. Blume has used her ear for adolescent dialogue, male and female, in many books for children over the years. The title heroine of *Deenie* (1973), who discovers she has scoliosis and has to wear a brace, is devastated because her physical impairment sets her apart from her peers, and she's convinced they will reject her. *Blubber* (1974) is the story of Linda, who is overweight and persecuted by her peers, a victim of the often unrealistic expectations of a looks-obsessed culture.

Blume became so popular with girls on the verge of adolescence that when she wrote *Forever* (1975), intended for young adults, younger girls also read it. Since it is a story about a teenager's decision to have sex with her boyfriend, many parents and librarians became concerned about its effect on younger readers. But the romance in the book is tempered by Blume's step-by-step descriptions of the sexual process, with emphasis on birth control and protection against sexual diseases. The book continues to be popular with today's teenagers, and adults who read it can appreciate its value as a sex-education tool.

Judy Blume filled a void in literature for girls, and the general public has responded enthusiastically to her books, but Blume's books alone will not act as the sustaining force to help a girl through adolescence. Blume delves into different issues, but her resolutions are either unrealistic or avoided altogether. Variety is the key.

CONTEMPORARY SERIES: SHALLOW CHARACTERS, PREDICTABLE PLOT

Books that feature strong young women who have preserved their own identity transmit a much deeper message to girls than books in the popular Goosebumps and Fear Street series by R.L. Stine, which offer shallow characterizations and minor roles for females. Stine's Kat in *It Came from Beneath the Sink!* (Goosebumps, 1995) and Corky in *Cheerleaders: The New Evil* (Fear Street, 1994) lack the qualities that would make them role models for girls. And because these books are as apt to be read by girls as by boys, the lack of character exhibited by the females confirms a female adolescent's lack of self-esteem.

Stine has made the comment "that kids as well as adults are entitled to books of no socially redeeming value." It's one thing to present stories that focus on action rather than character; it's quite another to present stories that not only label girls as almost totally dependent on boys but also present a cast of characters who show no remorse for wrongdoing. The overall attitude of the characters in Stine's books is, "Honestly, folks, it's not my fault." Parents might want to supplement these series with books that offer a more positive portrait of boys *and* girls. Chances are, the children themselves will start looking for more content in the books they read.

After reading a few Goosebumps and Fear Street books, the Baby-sitters Club series by Ann Martin is, at first, a welcome relief. It is, after all, a series in which girls have the leading roles. But a second look calls for further appraisal. While R.L. Stine prides himself on avoiding social redemption in his books, Martin's series offers interchangeable do-good characters who invariably learn at least one lesson, sometimes more. As in many series books, the characters are totally predictable. Each featured character reacts thoughtlessly to adversity, as in the Stine books, blaming someone else for her problems, but in contrast to the Stine books, Martin's characters finally realize the error of their ways. Even so, there is no spontaneity in these books, and although each member of the Baby-sitters Club is carefully assigned traits intended to set her apart from the rest, the girls are basically the same person, regardless of ethnic or social background.

Claudia, for example, is a Japanese-American member of the Baby-sitters Club, but in *Claudia and Crazy Peaches* (1994), any ethnic distinction that might exist within her family is ignored. Claudia, born an American, can't spell, eats lots of junk food, and has artistic talent. She is "a typical teenager," but Martin has overlooked the opportunity to show the cultural conflicts that sometimes occur within families when American values clash with the family's heritage.

Kristy is the president and founder of the Baby-sitters Club; in *Kristy and Mr. Mom* (1995), her family reflects contemporary America with sisters and brothers, stepsisters and stepbrothers, and even a four-year-old adopted sister from Vietnam. In the first book in the series, *Kristy's Great Idea* (1986), Kristy, whose mother is divorced and has to work outside the home, finds it difficult to juggle baby-sitting chores between family and neighborhood and has the idea to start a baby-sitters club with her friends. By the time of *Kristy and Mr. Mom,* Kristy's mother is married to a millionaire, who is also divorced with children, and the family has increased to 10 members, including Kristy's grandmother, who has taken on responsibility for domestic chores.

When Kristy's stepfather has a mild heart attack and decides to stop working and take over the running of the household, misunderstandings occur and chaos prevails until the family gets together and comes up with a solution. In this story, Kristy's mother has been relegated to the background, and it's not at all clear where she spends her days. Martin seems to be trying so hard to reflect a politically correct society, with a stepfather who shares household chores, a grandmother who is more active than passive, and a mother who is not limited to home and family, that the mother's role in the family is lost in the shuffle. The conflict occurs between Kristy's stepfather and her grandmother, with grandmother moving into her own apartment when it doesn't seem that she is needed any longer, then moving back when Kristy's stepfather admits he can't both run a household and handle increasing business duties. It's difficult to identify the role model in this book, if indeed there is one, unless it's the stepfather who finally accepts his own shortcomings and admits he can't do everything himself.

The American Girl Collection does a better job of differentiating between the various protagonists than the Babysitters Club series does, because each of the featured characters lives at a different time in American history. Every book, however, follows exactly the same format. The series was developed by the Pleasant Company, a small publisher in Wisconsin, and became so successful that it was picked up by Scholastic and widely distributed, with books, dolls, and accessories representing specific eras in American history. The books are written by and credited to a variety of authors, all of whom follow a preplanned story line that offers details of American society in the year assigned to each of six main characters: Felicity, Kirsten, Addy, Samantha, Molly and a new character, Josefina.

Samantha Learns a Lesson: A School Story (1986), by Susan S. Adler, is set in a small town called Mount Bedford in 1904. Samantha's world includes a wide gap between wealth and poverty, a continuing reliance on English mores, a prejudicial but growing education system, and many technological advances. At the end of the book, facts concerning the growth of the American education system in the early part of this century are presented with selected photographs from the period. Each book concludes with a similar summary of American history as it relates to the chosen theme, and the story line is deliberately educational. *Happy Birthday, Samantha! A Springtime Story* (1991) by Valerie Tripp includes a chapter about the efforts of Susan B. Anthony and other suffragists to gain voting rights for women. In this particular story, the focus on willingness to accept change takes over the story line, and Samantha is little more than an onlooker as those around her deal with the issues.

As a social studies supplement, the American Girl series presents history as experienced by the females of a particular era, offering a viewpoint that in past years has been ignored in history textbooks. As a guide to character development, however, the series falls short.

Series books have a tendency to lack character development because they are based on a recurring storyline that is predictable and unchanging. It is therefore not surprising that their popularity depends more on how soon the next book will come out than on how compelling the previous books might have been.

HOPE FOR THE FUTURE

Parents, teachers, and librarians are quick to criticize the series book, while many books that have found a niche as a literary classic, such as *Mr. Popper's Penguins* (1938), enjoy continued popularity no matter how old-fashioned or outdated their messages might be. As entertainment, *Mr. Popper's Penguins,* written by Richard Atwater and revised by his wife, Florence Atwater, appeals to middle-grade readers who appreciate its humor and the far-fetched adventures that result from having a penguin as a pet in a residential neighborhood. In a reflection of the time in which it was written, however, it portrays a less than positive view of female identity.

The Poppers live in a small city called Stillwater, and Mr. Popper is a house painter. He and his wife have two children, a girl and a boy, and like many in the Great Depression of the 1930s, the family struggles to get by, especially since Mr. Popper's job is seasonal. It is Mr. Popper's dream to go to the South Pole, but a letter to Admiral Drake instead brings a penguin to his home in Stillwater, a penguin who gets lonesome and needs a mate, and pretty soon the Poppers have not 2 but 12 penguins.

Mrs. Popper lacks a distinct identity. She accepts every decision her husband makes and devotes her life to her family. While she does her mending, Mr. Popper reads travel books. She does the marketing and frequently has to clean up after her husband, children, and penguins, but she gets no help from her out-of-work husband.

Shallow characterizations of females in children's books do little to increase the prestige of women, and far too many popular children's books have a tendency to relegate girls to a lesser role. Such oversights increase the value of books that feature heroic females in roles that give them equal status and confirm their value in society.

Fortunately, children's books in general have reached a higher level of sophistication in the last decades of this century, and books that offer layers of meaning are more common today. With academics beginning to include children's literature in their studies, there is more demand for quality, for plain good writing, than on what lessons a children's book might teach. Early children's books that have lasted as originally written are those in which character development and artistic use of language create multiple levels of meaning, calling for further exploration of content.

Where Have the Books for Boys Gone?

Stefan Kanfer

Stefan Kanfer, a highly esteemed biographer, writer, and editor, was a journalist at *Time* magazine for over twenty years. He believes that the publishing industry is doing today's boys a disservice. Under the banner of political correctness, adventure tales, patriotic stories, and magical fantasies are being replaced by watered down social dramas about getting along with others. Kanfer feels that this "feminization" of children's literature is a potentially damaging trend since little boys are left with no outlet for their innate desire for adventure and their need for strong male role models. Fortunately, as Kanfer notes, male-centered books have not yet disappeared and new arrivals, like J.K. Rowling's Harry Potter series, are giving boys the role models and adventure they need.

Buying a book for a 6-year-old boy ought to be a no-brainer. Go to the nearest bookstore, find the children's section, and grab something that you liked when you were that age. Or so I thought when I plunked down $12 for a copy of *The Little Engine That Could.*

When I got home I flipped through the pages. The illustrations and typeface were reassuring; I remembered them from childhood. Then I came across this sentence: "She brought toys to all the good little boys and girls."

She brought? SHE? This thrusting locomotive, one of the most obvious phallic symbols in the lexicon, was now female?

This prompted me to do some research. As it turns out, that Little Engine started out almost a century ago as an it— "It sighed, 'I think I can, I think I can.'" Then the machine became male. Then there were male and female versions, in keeping with the New Ungendered Sensitivity. It was downhill from there. Try to find a Little Engine referred to as "he" today. That version is no longer in print.

PUBLISHERS GEAR MORE BOOKS TO GIRLS TODAY

I went back to the store and found my worst fears confirmed. Publishers, like politicians, read polls. They are keenly aware that mothers, not fathers, buy most kid lit. So even when the works are supposed to be for young males, the bookmakers aim their output at mature females. Thus, what might be called the "feminization" of kid literature. We get fewer adventure and war stories, and more about getting along. We get more tales about feelings and fewer about facts. We get many, many stories like the one about a boy who had the courage to take ballet lessons when all the other guys were out playing softball.

The uncomfortable truth is that boys' books are too important to be left to mothers and librarians. Fathers have to get in on the act, because they understand boys and their needs in ways that mothers can't—not just their appetite for adventure, but their need for exemplars of heroism and valor.

Until recently, this was a given. Boys growing up in the '50s and '60s had the time-honored Hardy Boys series for a sense of adventure and gentlemanly macho. The Landmark series, featuring such titles as *Guadalcanal Diary* and *The Pirate Lafitte and the Battle of New Orleans,* offered stirring accounts of historical heroism. They bred respect for patriotism and other currently derided virtues.

And, of course, before that there were such tales as Rudyard Kipling's *Kim,* about a boy who has to find his own way during the dangerous days of the British Raj; Robert Louis Stevenson's *Treasure Island* and *Kidnapped;* and Thomas Bailey Aldrich's *The Story of a Bad Boy,* a funny account of a kid growing up in nineteenth-century America.

But Kipling is now considered the bard of imperialism, and so his virile, brilliant prose and poetry have nearly vanished from bookstores catering to the young. Stevenson's novels have fallen out of favor, at least in part because they feature minors using guns and tobacco. And Aldrich's protagonist is a middle-class youngster from an intact family. In the day of the single parent, it has obviously been deemed irrelevant.

The removal of such stories from contemporary boyhood has taken its toll, since those tales inspired and gave moral direction. At last, belatedly, we are starting to realize that it is boys who are in the most trouble today. They are almost 12 times more likely than girls to drop out of high school, and there are more than twice as many boys as girls in high school special-ed classes. Young men are six times more likely than young women to commit suicide.

BOYS NEED BETTER BOOKS

Obviously, curing these ills will require more than simply providing better reading material for boys. But reform has to begin somewhere, and we can start by stiff-arming the lousy books others would foist on our kids. I well remember my own struggle with junk lit when my children were small. That was in the early '70s, when a fatuous volume called *Free to Be You and Me* was published. The anthology was put together by that profound analytical thinker Marlo Thomas. It contained a number of tales, poems, and commentaries by the likes of Gloria Steinem. Among the contents was a song for boys entitled "It's All Right to Cry." There was also a narrative assuring parents that not only was it okay for boys to have dolls, but they should be encouraged to do so. Somebody gave my children a copy. I traded it in for a collection of Grimm's Fairy Tales the next day.

Kid lit has gone mainly downhill from there. The majority of works today carry the same boring and bogus messages: All people are the same. No one should ever feel bad. The most dangerous word in the language is "judgmental." These books' sorriest feature is not their doggedly PC agenda. It is the assumption that the child is a miniature adult who is actually helped by a stack of nonthreatening, feel-good volumes.

The psychologist Bruno Bettelheim knew better. In *The Uses of Enchantment,* still the best book ever written about children's literature, he praises stories with unambiguous heroes and harsh villains. Bettelheim made the Grimm Brothers the centerpiece of his argument. For him, the German poet Schiller had said it all: "Deeper meaning resides in the fairy tales told to me in my childhood than in the truth that is taught by life."

I'll buy that. My father read those tales to me, and I read them to my son. Innately, we all discerned their value, not only in getting a kid to sleep but in guiding him through life. And with good reason. The narratives have the strength accumulated by their passage through the generations. They retain such power because a child—particularly a boy—still sees life in the melodramatic terms of a fairy tale. To a boy, the protagonist who has to ascend the glass mountain, slay the fire-breathing dragon, and banish the witch is not merely a medieval adventurer. He is also the reader, learning to stick up for himself.

But there's no point in complaining about the feminization of children's literature if we fathers and grandfathers don't turn the polls on their ears. How? By wielding the weapons at hand—the wallet and the credit card—to buy strong, intelligent, unpropagandized books for our boys.

The good news is that despite efforts to excise good male-oriented literature, a lot of it is still out there. Sometimes the books are even written by women—as in the case of the Harry Potter series, creations of a gifted British woman who goes by J.K. Rowling.

I know of no better endorsement for these stories than this: The South Carolina Board of Education is considering a ban on Harry Potter in the classroom. "The books have a serious tone of death, hate, lack of respect, and sheer evil," complained one parent who recently addressed the board. And in Georgia, an elementary-school principal named Jerry Locke said, "It's questionable whether every parent wants their child to read or be exposed to books having to do with magic and wizardry."

I have a bulletin for these would-be censors. Boys need magic and wizardry in order to grow up. Television can't supply enough of it, and neither can the movies. Special effects are no match for scenes in the mind's eye. The kid who reads is his own director, set designer, cinematographer, and star.

The authors of the great classics for boys knew that the young read in a different way from their parents. Isaac Bashevis Singer said it best when he accepted the Nobel Prize in literature a generation ago: "There are 500 reasons why I began to write for children," he told his audience. For brevity's sake, we can stick with one: "They don't expect their beloved writer to redeem humanity. Young as they are, they know that it is not in his power. Only the adults have such childish illusions."

Harry Potter and the Question of Magic

Alan Jacobs

The most talked about children's books at the end
of the twentieth century were J.K. Rowling's Harry
Potter novels. Alan Jacobs, an English professor at
Wheaton College in Illinois, discusses the popularity of the series, and examines the significance of
the controversy surrounding them. Unlike some educators and religious leaders, he doesn't believe
that the books—which revolve around a teenage
wizard—should be kept from children because of
their subject matter.

By now most readers in this country are aware of what has
come to be called the Harry Potter phenomenon. It's hard to
be unaware. Any bookstore you might care to enter is strewn
with giant stacks of the Harry Potter books—three of them
now that *Harry Potter and the Prisoner of Azkaban* has finally been released in the United States. This blessed event
comes after some months during which the on-line bookstore Amazon.co.uk—Britain's branch of the ever-expanding
Amazon.com empire—devoted much of its energy to ship-
ping copies across the Atlantic, creating in the process a
miniature trade war, as lawyers on both sides of the pond
tried to figure out which country a book is purchased in
when it's ordered *from* a British company but *on* a computer
in America. Whatever the legal status of cyberspatial commerce, anyone visiting either Amazon.com or Amazon.co.uk
last summer could not but note that the best-selling books
on both sites were the Harry Potter novels, which ranked a
consistent one, two, and three.

Many people are also familiar with the story behind the
most talked-about children's books in decades, perhaps ever:
how Joanne Rowling, an out-of-work teacher and single

Excerpted from Alan Jacobs, "*Harry Potter*'s Magic," *First Things*, January 2000.
Reprinted with permission from *First Things*.

mother living on the dole in Edinburgh, started scribbling a story in a local café as her small daughter dozed in a stroller; how an English publisher, Bloomsbury Books, took a chance on this unknown author; and how, almost wholly by word-of-mouth reports. The first novel, *Harry Potter and the Philosopher's Stone*, became a best-seller not just among children but also among adults, for whom Bloomsbury designed a more mature-looking cover so commuters on bus and tube would not have to be embarrassed as they eagerly followed Harry's quest to discover what the enormous three-headed dog, Fluffy, was guarding in that off-limits corridor of Hogwarts School of Witchcraft and Wizardry. International success, as indicated by those great piles of books at 40 percent discount and the dominance of Amazon's best-seller lists, quickly followed.

ROWLING, THE WORLD-MAKER

In the twenty-some-odd years that I have been pretty closely following trends in American publishing, no development in the industry has been nearly so inexplicable to me, nor has any development made me so happy. For I adore the Harry Potter books. I read the first one—under its silly American title, *Harry Potter and the Sorcerer's Stone* (the American publisher evidently judged that no book with the word "philosopher" in the title could sell)—thinking that it might be something I could read to my son. Though I decided that he wasn't quite old enough, at six, to follow the rather complicated plot, I myself was hooked, and in my impatience ordered each of the next two novels in the series from Amazon.co.uk, thus making my own personal contribution to the perplexity of international trade law. (The remaining books in the series—Rowling plans a total of seven—will be published simultaneously in the U.S. and the U.K., thus cutting the legal Gordian knot.)

J.K. Rowling, as the books' covers have it—the name rhymes with "bowling"—simply has that mysterious gift, so prized among storytellers and lovers of stories but so resistant to critical explication, of world-making. It is a gift that many Christian readers tend to associate with that familiar but rather amorphous group of English Christian writers, the Inklings—though the association is not quite proper, since only one of the Inklings, J.R.R. Tolkien, had this rare faculty, and few of the others even aspired to it. Tolkien, however, possessed the power in spades, and gave useful names to it as well: he spoke of the "secondary worlds" created by the writer, and of "mythopoeia" as the activity of such "sub-creation." The sine qua non of such mythopoeia, for Tolkien, is the making of a world that resembles ours but is not ours, a world that possesses internal logic and self-consistency to the same degree that ours does—but not the *same* logic: it must have its own rules, rules that are peculiar to it and that generate consequences also peculiar to it.

It is important to understand that C.S. Lewis' Narnia books, great though they may be, are not in this strict sense mythopoeic: Lewis does not want to create a self-consistent secondary world, but rather a world in which all the varieties of mythology meet and find their home. In Narnia there is no internal consistency whatever: thus Father Christmas can show up in the middle of *The Lion, the Witch, and the Wardrobe,* and Bacchus and Silenus in the middle of *Prince Caspian.* It may well be that this mythographic promiscuity, so to speak, is key to the success of the Chronicles of Narnia, but it makes them very different books from Tolkien's, and it is the reason why Tolkien hated the Narnia stories. They lacked the clearly demarcated wholeness which he considered the essential virtue of his own Middle Earth.

Joanne Rowling has expressed her love for the Narnia books—one of the reasons there will be, God willing, seven Harry Potter books is that there are seven volumes of Narnia stories—but as a literary artist she bears a far greater resemblance to Tolkien. One of the great pleasures for the reader of her books is the wealth of details, from large to small, that mark the Magic world as different from ours (which in the books is called the Muggle world): the tall pointed hats the students wear in their classes, in which they study such topics as Potions, Transfiguration, Defense Against the Dark Arts, and even Care and Feeding of Magical Creatures: the spells that are always in Latin (*"Expelliarmus!"*); or the universal addiction to Quidditch, a game that shares some characteristics with basketball, cricket, and soccer but is played in the air, on broomsticks, and with four balls. Rowling's attention to such matters is remarkable and charming, especially when the details are small: once, when he is visiting the home of a friend from a Magical family, Harry steps over a pack of Self-Shuffling Playing Cards. It's an item that could have been left out without any loss to the narrative, but it offers an elegant little surprise—and another piece of furniture for this thoroughly imagined universe.

SORCERY THEME CAUSES CONTROVERSY

I have made my enthusiasm for these books quite evident to many friends, but some of them are dubious—indeed, deeply suspicious. These are Christian people, and they feel that books which make magic so funny and charming don't exactly support the Christian view of things. Such novels could at best encourage children to take a smilingly tolerant New Age view of witchcraft, at worst encourage the practice of witchcraft itself. Moreover, some of them note, Harry Potter is not exactly a model student: he has, as the Headmaster of Hogwarts puts it, "a certain disregard for rules," and spends a good deal of time fervently hoping not to get caught in mid-disregard.

This second matter, I think, poses no real problem. It is true that Harry is often at odds with some of his teachers, but these particular teachers are not exactly admirable figures: they themselves are often at odds with the wise, benevolent, and powerful Headmaster, Albus Dumbledore, whom they sometimes attempt to undermine or outflank. But to Dumbledore, significantly, Harry is unswervingly faithful and obedient: indeed, the climax of the second novel, *Harry Potter and the Chamber of Secrets,* turns on Harry's fidelity to Dumbledore.

Moreover, Harry's tendency to bypass or simply flout the rules is a matter of moral concern for him: he wonders and worries about the self-justifications he offers, and often doubts not just his abilities but his virtue. He is constantly aware that his great unchosen antagonist, Voldemort—the Dark Lord, the most evil of wizards and, after Dumbledore, the most powerful—offers temptations to which he cannot simply assume that he is immune. And when Dumbledore mentions Harry's "certain disregard for rules" he does so in a way that links such disregard with the forces of evil, thus warning Harry (though his larger purpose in that scene is to encourage the troubled young wizard).

In short, Rowling's moral compass throughout the three novels is sound—indeed, I would say, acute. But the matter of witchcraft remains, and it is not a matter to be trifled with. People today, and this includes many Christians, tend to hold two views about witches: first, that real witches don't exist, and second, that they aren't as bad as the evil master-minds of the Salem witch trials made them out to be. These are obviously incompatible beliefs. As C.S. Lewis has pointed out, there is no virtue in being tolerant of witches if you think that witchcraft is impossible, that is, that witches don't really exist. But if there are such things as witches, and they do indeed invoke supernatural or unnatural forces to bring harm to good people, then it would be neither wise nor good to tolerate them. So the issue is an important one, and worthy of serious reflection.

It is tempting to say, in response to these concerns, that Harry Potter is not that kind of wizard, that he doesn't do harm to anyone, except those who are manifestly evil and trying to do harm to him. And these are significant points. But an answer to our question must begin elsewhere.

PUTTING WITCHCRAFT IN CONTEXT

The place to begin is to invoke one of the great achievements of twentieth-century historical scholarship: the eight volumes Lynn Thorndike published between 1929 and 1941 under the collective title *A History of Magic and Experimental Science*. And it is primarily the title that I wish to reflect upon here. In the thinking of most modern people, there should be two histories here: after all, are not magic and experimental science opposites? Is not magic governed by superstition, ignorance, and wishful thinking, while experimental science is rigorous, self-critical, and methodological? While it may be true that the two paths have diverged to the point that they no longer have any point of contact, for much of their existence—and this is Lynn Thorndike's chief point—they constituted a single path with a single history. For both magic and experimental science are means of controlling and directing our natural environment (and people insofar as they are part of that environment). C.S. Lewis has made the same assertion:

> [Francis Bacon's] endeavor is no doubt contrasted in our minds with that of the magicians: but contrasted only in the light of the event, only because we know that science succeeded and magic failed. That event was then still uncertain. Stripping off our knowledge of it, we see at once that Bacon and the magicians have the closest possible affinity. . . . Nor would Bacon himself deny the affinity: he thought the aim of the magicians was "noble."

It was not obvious in advance that science would succeed

and magic fail: in fact, several centuries of dedicated scientific experiment would have to pass before it was clear to anyone that the "scientific" physician could do more to cure illness than the old woman of the village with her herbs and potions and muttered charms. In the Renaissance, alchemists were divided between those who sought to solve problems—the achievement of the philosopher's stone, for example (or should I say the *sorcerer's* stone?)—primarily through the use of what we would call mixtures of chemicals and those who relied more heavily on incantations, the drawing of mystical patterns, and the invocation of spirits.

HARRY POTTER SETS RECORDS

The Palm Beach Post *reports the various ways the Harry Potter books have influenced the children's publishing industry in America.*

How popular are the Harry Potter children's books? So popular that they are driving up the sales of children's literature.

• In 1999, paperback sales of children's books increased almost 24 percent to $660 million. Hardcover sales grew more than 11 percent to $1.6 billion. In contrast, hardcover sales for adults increased only 2.6 percent and paperback sales grew about 3 percent.

• Last month, five children's novels—three of them Harry Potter books—were at the top of *The New York Times* bestseller list. The *Times* may create a separate children's list in response.

• The Potter craze is helping increase the sales of older children's classics, especially ones with a British background like Potter, such as C.S. Lewis' Chronicles of Narnia series.

"Thank You, Harry Potter!" *Palm Beach Post*, March 12, 2000.

At least, it seems to *us* that the alchemists can be so divided. But that's because we know that one approach developed into chemistry, while the other became pure magic. The division may not have been nearly so evident at the time, when (to adapt Weber's famous phrase) the world had not yet become disenchanted. As Keith Thomas has shown, it was "the triumph of the mechanical philosophy" of nature that "meant the end of the animistic conception of the universe which had constituted the basic rationale for magical thinking." Even after powerful work of the mechanistic scientists like Gassendi the change was not easily completed: Isaac Newton, whose name is associated more than any other with physical mechanics, dabbled frequently in alchemy.

MAGIC AND TECHNOLOGY

This history provides a key to understanding the role of magic in Joanne Rowling's books, for she begins by positing a counterfactual history, a history in which magic was not a false and incompetent discipline, but rather a means of controlling the physical world at least as potent as experimental science. In Harry Potter's world, scientists think of magic in precisely the same way they do in our world, but they are wrong. The counterfactual "secondary world" that Rowling creates is one in which magic simply works, and works as reliably, in the hands of a trained wizard, as the technology that makes airplanes fly and refrigerators chill the air—those products of applied science being, by the way, sufficiently inscrutable to the people who use them that they might as well be the products of wizardry. As Arthur C. Clarke once wrote, "Any smoothly functioning technology gives the appearance of magic."

The fundamental moral framework of the Harry Potter books, then, is a familiar one to all of us: it is the problem of technology. (As Jacques Ellul wrote, "Magic may even be the origin of techniques.") Hogwarts School of Witchcraft and Wizardry is in the business of teaching people how to harness and employ certain powers—that they are powers unrecognized by science is really beside the point—but cannot insure that people will use those powers wisely, responsibly, and for the common good. It is a choice, as the thinkers of the Renaissance would have put it, between *magia* and *goetia*: "high magic" (like the wisdom possessed by the magi in Christian legend) and "dark magic."

Hogwarts was founded by four wizards, one of whom, Salazar Slytherin, at least dabbled and perhaps reveled in the Dark Arts, that is, the use of his powers for questionable if not downright evil purposes, and for centuries many of the young wizards who reside in Slytherin House have exhibited the same tendency. The educational quandary for Albus Dumbledore, then—though it is never described so overtly—is how to train students not just in the "technology" of magic but also in the moral discernment necessary to avoid the continual reproduction of the few great Dark Lords like Voldemort and their multitudinous followers. The problem is exacerbated by the presence of faculty members who are not wholly unsympathetic with Voldemort's aims.

HARRY POTTER COMES OF AGE

The clarity with which Rowling sees the need to choose between good and evil is admirable, but still more admirable, to my mind, is her refusal to allow a simple division of parties into the Good and the Evil. Harry Potter is unquestionably a good boy, but, as I have suggested, a key component of his virtue arises from his recognition that he is not *inevitably* good. When first-year students arrive at Hogwarts, they come to an assembly of the entire school, students and faculty. Each of them sits on a stool in the midst of the assembly and puts on a large, battered, old hat—the Sorting Hat, which decides which of the four houses the student will enter. After unusually long reflection, the Sorting Hat, to Harry's great relief, puts him in Gryffindor, but not before telling him that he could achieve real greatness in Slytherin. This comment haunts Harry: he often wonders if Slytherin is where he truly belongs, among the pragmatists, the careerists, the manipulators and deceivers, the power-hungry, and the just plain nasty. Near the end of the second book, after a terrifying encounter with Voldemort—his third, since Voldemort had tried to kill Harry, and succeeded in killing his parents, when Harry was a baby, and had confronted Harry again in the first book—he confesses his doubts to Dumbledore.

"So I *should* be in Slytherin," Harry said, looking desperately into Dumbledore's face. "The Sorting Hat could see Slytherin's power in me, and it—"

"Put you in Gryffindor," said Dumbledore calmly. "Listen to me, Harry. You happen to have many qualities Salazar Slytherin prized in his hand-picked students. Resourcefulness . . . determination . . . a certain disregard for rules," he added, his moustache quivering again. "Yet the Sorting Hat placed you in Gryffindor. You know why that was. Think."

"It only put me in Gryffindor," said Harry in a defeated voice, "Because I asked not to go in Slytherin. . . ."

"Exactly," said Dumbledore, beaming once more. "Which makes you very different from [Voldemort]. It is our choices, Harry, that show what we truly are, far more than our abilities." Harry sat motionless in his chair, stunned.

Harry is stunned because he realizes for the first time that his confusion has been wrongheaded from the start: he has been asking the question "Who am I at heart?" when he needed to be asking the question "What must I do in order to become what I should be?" His character is not a fixed pre-existent thing, but something that he has the responsibility for making: that's why the Greeks called it character, "that which is engraved." It's also what the Germans mean when they speak of *Bildung,* and the Harry Potter books are of course a multivolume *Bildungsroman*—a story of "education," that is to say, of character formation.

In this sense the strong tendency of magic to become a dream of power—on the importance of this point Lynn Thorndike, Keith Thomas, and C.S. Lewis all agree—makes it a wonderful means by which to focus the theme of *Bildung,* of the choices that gradually but inexorably shape us into certain distinct kinds of persons. Christians are perhaps right to be wary of an overly positive portrayal of magic, but the Harry Potter books don't do that: in them magic is often fun, often surprising and exciting, but also always potentially dangerous.

And so, it should be said, is the technology that has resulted from the victory of experimental science. Perhaps the most important question I could ask my Christian friends who mistrust the Harry Potter books is this: is your concern about the portrayal of this imaginary magical technology matched by a concern for the effects of the technology that in our world displaced magic? The technocrats of this world hold in their hands powers almost infinitely greater than those of Albus Dumbledore and Voldemort: how worried are we about them, and their influence over our children? Not worried enough, I would say. As Ellul suggests, the task for us is "the measuring of technique by other criteria than those of technique itself," which measuring he also calls "the search for justice before God." Joanne Rowling's books are more helpful than most in prompting such measurement. They are also—and let's not forget the importance of this point—a great deal of fun.

The Continuing Need for Multicultural Literature

James S. Jacobs and Michael O. Tunnell

James S. Jacobs and Michael O. Tunnell are professors at Brigham Young University and coauthors of the book *Children's Literature, Briefly.* In a world full of fear and mistrust of people from different cultures, the authors stress the need for children to have access to multicultural and international literature at a very young age. They trace the rise of multicultural literature, identify its characteristics, and convey the importance the books play in opening children's minds and hearts.

Multicultural and international books offer positive experiences to young readers in at least three ways. Books about specific cultures and nations can:
- Foster an awareness, understanding, and appreciation of people who seem at first glance different from the reader
- Present a positive and reassuring representation of a reader's own cultural group
- Introduce readers to the literary traditions of different world cultures or cultural groups in America

Well-written books that express multicultural themes or are international in their origins may have a profound effect on readers, prompting a global outlook as well as an understanding that members of the human family have more similarities than differences.

DEFINING MULTICULTURAL LITERATURE

Multicultural books typically focus on so-called parallel cultures. Fiction involves main characters from minority groups; nonfiction focuses on the lives of real people from parallel cultures. Multicultural literature has often been equated with books about people of color, especially within the United States and Canada: African Americans, Native Americans, Asian Americans, Hispanics. However, this definition is far too narrow. Our diverse population includes a variety of cultural groups that often cross color lines, such as religious groups. Jews, Catholics, Moslems, Mormons, and the Amish all have their own subcultures and often have been misunderstood and even persecuted for their beliefs. As an example of books promoting understanding among religious factions, many Jewish students have expressed both interest and pleasure in reading Barbara Robinson's *The Best Christmas Pageant Ever.* Some students said they had always wondered about the Christian Christmas tradition of the pageant and Robinson's book made understandable what was strange to them—the story helped to bridge a cultural gap. Individuals with intellectual or physical disabilities also deserve books that represent them in honest, positive ways. For example, some deaf individuals consider themselves part of the Deaf Culture and are concerned about how the rest of society misunderstands them.

THE NEED FOR MULTICULTURAL BOOKS

Xenophobia, the mistrust or fear of people who are strangers or foreigners, is the root of our worldwide inability to live together in peace. Parents and society may purposely or inadvertently program children to mistrust, fear, or even hate certain groups of people who are unlike them. Teaching children at an early age "about the [positive] differences and similarities between people will not singularly ensure a more gentle and tolerant society, but might act as a prerequisite to one," [says educator Thomas Sobol]. Candy Dawson Boyd (1990) makes it clear that we cannot begin too early to give our children a multicultural perspective:

> We know that there's a substantial body of research on the development of racial consciousness begun in 1929, and what does it tell us? It tells us that children develop negative attitudes towards other people as they take on the culture of their parents. It tells us that by age three, racial awareness is evident. *Three.* And that by age ten, racial attitudes have crystallized.

Yet, children in early adolescence [Frances Sonneschein notes] "are not too old for significant attitudinal change. Counteraction is therefore possible. . . ."

Literature can be one of the most powerful tools for combating the ignorance that breeds xenophobic behavior. [Educator Nancy Hansen-Krening points out,] "for decades experienced educators have reported success stories about using children's literature to broaden attitudes toward people from a variety of cultures." Rudine Sims Bishop, who has long been a champion of the well-written multicultural book, believes that "literature is one of the most powerful components of a multicultural education curriculum, the underlying purpose of which is to help make the society a more equitable one." In support of this view, she quotes James Baldwin: "Literature is indispensable to the world. . . . The world changes according to the way people see it, and if you alter, even by a millimeter, the way a person looks at reality, then you can change it." Indeed, studies have indicated that students' prejudices have been reduced because of their involvement with good multicultural books.

Certainly, children of minority cultural groups need books that bolster self-esteem and pride in their heritage. And children of all groups, especially majority children, need books that sensitize them to people from cultural groups different from their own.

JUDGING MULTICULTURAL LITERATURE

As with all books, multicultural books ought to measure up to the criteria used to judge literature in general. However, additional criteria focusing on the multicultural themes and content are also necessary to consider.

- Racial or cultural stereotyping must be avoided. Stereotypes are alienating because they perpetuate a simplified, biased, and often negative view of groups of people: All African Americans are poor, all Hispanics are lazy, all Asians are secretive and sly, all Jews are born entrepreneurs. Though common elements often link the lives and daily practices of members of a cultural group, it is important to communicate that every group is made up of individuals who have their own sets of personal values, attitudes, and beliefs. In books written for children, characters who are cultural minorities need to be represented as true individuals, and a positive image needs to be presented. However, this still leaves room for showing both positive and negative behaviors in minority as well as majority group characters. For instance, in the Newbery-winning novel, *Roll of Thunder, Hear My Cry,* a story of racial prejudice in Mississippi of the 1930s, Mildred Taylor creates African American characters who represent a broad spectrum of human characteristics. Cassie Logan is proud and honorable, though a bit stubborn. T.J. is weak and dishonest. By the same token, Taylor does not make all whites racial bigots.

- Cultural details need to be represented accurately in literature. These may include the use of dialects or idioms; descriptions of ethnic foods, customs, and clothing; and religious beliefs and practices. Of course, sensitivity to subcultures within a group is also important. For example, customs vary among the different factions of Judaism; Hasidic Jews are strictly orthodox as evidenced by dress codes and other identifiable practices, but Reform Jews are much less bound by religious law. In the same way, customs and lifestyles vary greatly among the many Native American tribes.

- Cultural authenticity is a sensitive issue in children's literature today. Many people feel that books examining a specific culture should not be written by someone who is an outsider. For instance, the Newbery-winning novel *Sounder* by William Armstrong portrays the lives of a poor family of African American sharecroppers. Armstrong is not an African American, and critics charge that there is no way he could understand the nuances of living in this culture. "Someone who does not share the specifics of a culture remains an outsider, no matter how astute a student or how well-meaning their intentions," [believes critic August Wilson]. Worse yet, some critics maintain that many multicultural books written by outsiders provide a distorted view because the author is biased or culturally prejudiced.

At the same time, others believe that if outsiders make concentrated efforts not only to understand but also to inhabit a different cultural world, then they may indeed be able to write with cultural authenticity. Of course, some rare authors seem to have a particular gift for "imagining other's lives." For instance, Miriam Horn makes a case for Eudora Welty's uncanny ability:

> "Miss Eudora" could . . . enter into the stolid, exhausted body of an old black woman or let loose with a bluesy tale as full of tumbles and howls as a Fats Waller jam. Before she was 30, she could feel the frantic loneliness of a middle-

aged traveling salesman. . . . She could even, on the hot night in 1963 that civil-rights leader Medgar Evers was killed, transform her own soft, lilting voice into the bitter ranting of a hate-filled assassin. Of the story she wrote that night in the voice of the murderer she says: "You have to give any human being the right to have you use your imagination about them."

Whoever the author, it is of great importance to have books for young readers that are culturally authentic.

• Awareness about the types of multicultural books that exist may be helpful in judging and selecting books for libraries and classrooms. Certainly they include folktales, biographies, historical novels, informational books, fantasy, picture books, and contemporary realistic novels. However, Rudine Sims Bishop suggests that there are three general categories of books about people of color: neutral, generic, and specific. In many instances, these categories also could be applied to other cultural groups.

Culturally neutral children's books include characters from cultural minorities but are essentially about other topics. Sims [Bishop] says that this variety is mostly made up of picture books and gives the example of a book about medical examinations wherein "a Japanese-American child might be shown visiting the doctor, who might be an African-American female." Neutral books randomly place multicultural faces among the pages in order to make a statement about the value of diversity.

Generic books focus on characters representing a cultural group, but few specific details are included that aid in developing a cultural persona. Instead, these characters are functioning in the books as regular people existing in a large common culture, such as American culture. A classic example is the Caldecott-winning *The Snowy Day* by Ezra Jack Keats, which features an African American family living in an inner city. The book shows a black child enjoying newly fallen snow, just as any other child might. Although this book is noted as one of the first books to have an African American child as a protagonist, some critics feel that the child's mother is presented as a stereotypical black woman—the large, loving Negro mammy image. Despite the fact that this variety of multicultural book contains little culturally specific material, concerned readers still scrutinize the books hoping to find characters with realistic, nonstereotypical qualities.

Culturally specific children's books incorporate specific cultural details that help define characters. Cultural themes are evident if not prevailing in fictional plots or nonfiction content. Of course, in picture books the artwork will express many of these cultural details. It is in this category of multicultural literature that cultural authenticity is particularly important. The recommended reading list at the conclusion of this chapter is organized by cultural divisions and presents books considered to be both quality literature and culturally authentic.

THE GROWTH OF MULTICULTURAL LITERATURE

Children's books in the past generally treated minority groups badly or ignored them completely. However, when African American author Arna Bontemps won a Newbery Honor Award in 1949 for *Story of the Negro* and became the first African American to appear on the Newbery list, he ushered in the real beginnings of change for all cultural groups. Though few other minority authors or illustrators appeared on award lists during the next two decades, more of their work was being produced. Also, books by majority culture authors that presented less stereotypical images of minority cultures appeared and received awards: *Song of the Swallows* by Leo Politi won the Caldecott Award in 1950 and was the first Caldecott winner with a Hispanic American protagonist; *Amos Fortune, Free Man* by Elizabeth Yates, *Secret of the Andes* by Ann Nolan Clark, and . . . *And Now Miguel* by Joseph Krumgold won the Newbery Award in 1951, 1953, and 1954 respectively; and *The Snowy Day* by Ezra Jack Keats won the Caldecott in 1963.

As the Civil Rights movement gained momentum in the 1960s, awareness of and sensitivity to minorities increased. In 1965 the literary world was awakened by the publication of a startling article titled "The All White World of Children's Books." Printed in the *Saturday Review* and written by Nancy Larrick, this article reported that almost no African Americans appeared in any of America's children's books. The publishing and library worlds took notice, and efforts to include more African Americans in children's books eventually blossomed to include other racial minorities, women, people with physical and mental disadvantages, and other groups. In 1966 the Council on Interracial Books for Children (CIBC) was founded. Its publication pointed to racial stereotypes still appearing in children's books, and its efforts with publishers helped promote and get into print the works of authors and illustrators of color, particularly African Americans. In fact, for a number of years the CIBC sponsored an annual contest for unpublished writers and illustrators of color and saw to it that the winners' works were published. The authors and illustrators who were given their start by the CIBC are some of the best-known today in the world of multicultural children's literature: African American authors Mildred Taylor and Walter Dean Myers, Native American author Virginia Driving Hawk Sneve, and Asian American writers Ai-Ling Louie and Minfong Ho. In 1969 the Coretta Scott King Award was established to recognize the distinguished work of African American writers and illustrators. Then in 1975, Virginia Hamilton won the Newbery Award for *M.C. Higgins the Great,* the first African American to be so honored. The next year Leo Dillon became the first African American to win the Caldecott Medal, an award he shared with his wife, Diane, who is not black, for their illustrations in *Why Mosquitoes Buzz in People's Ears,* written by Verna Aardema.

Since the 1960s more authors from minority cultural and racial groups have been writing for children and appear consistently on best-books lists and awards lists. Still, there is much room for growth in this area of publishing. More minority titles and writers are needed, particularly Hispanic and Native American, and books representing the intellectually and physically disabled cultures. However, the call has been issued, and in time we hope that the void will be filled.

BROADENING THE SCOPE: INTERNATIONAL BOOKS

Just as multicultural books dealing with American society assist in creating a bridge of understanding, international books can help children gain an appreciation and understanding of our global society. The history and culture of other countries as well as their literary traditions are illuminated through books that have their origins outside the United States.

The most common international books in the United States are English-language titles written and published in another English-speaking country, such as England, Canada,

Australia, and New Zealand. Because these books need no translation, they can be acquired and marketed readily by American publishers.

Although translated books are less plentiful in this country, this area of publishing is growing. These foreign-language books originally had been written and printed in other countries. American companies then acquire the rights to publish them, and they are translated into English. A limited number of foreign-language children's books from other countries are released in the United States in untranslated form.

One consideration when judging translated books is the quality of the translation. Though the flavor of the country needs to be retained, the English text must be fluent and readable, yet not too "Americanized." Often a few foreign words and phrases may be left in to provide readers a feel for the culture and language, but too many can be troublesome for children.

There is an ever-increasing exchange of children's books among countries, but most of the international books published in the United States come from Europe. Each year since 1966, publishers from around the world have attended an international children's book fair in Bologna, Italy, where they share their books with one another and work out agreements for publishing them in other countries.

Since World War II, a number of organizations, publications, and awards have been established to promote the idea of an international world of children's books. In 1949, the International Youth Library was founded in Munich, Germany. It has become a world center for the study of children's literature. In 1953, the International Board on Books for Young People (IBBY) was established, and soon after, in 1956, this organization created the first international children's book award. The Hans Christian Andersen Medal is given every two years to an author whose lifetime contribution to the world of children's literature is considered outstanding. In 1966, a separate award for illustration was added to the Hans Christian Medal, and IBBY also began publishing *Bookbird*, a journal linking those interested in international children's books. In 1968 in the United States, the American Library Association began presenting the Mildred Batchelder Award to the American publisher of the most noteworthy translated children's book of the year.

With the increased emphasis on well-written multicultural and international children's books, teachers and parents have another means by which they may help children avoid the pitfalls of ignorance that breed intolerance, hatred, and conflict. In an atomic age, we certainly cannot afford the increasingly deadly outcomes sparked by xenophobic behaviors.

CHRONOLOGY

1484

Aesop's Fables, published in English by William Caxton, is one of the first books to be printed after the invention of the printing press.

1657

Orbis Pictus (*Illustrated World*) by Johann Amos Comenius is the first children's picture book.

1691

The New England Primer teaches moral lessons to Puritan children in America.

1719

Robinson Crusoe by Daniel Defoe is beloved by children though written for adults.

1729

Tales of Mother Goose by Charles Perrault is published in English; it is the first legitimate book of fairy tales and nursery rhymes.

1736

Gulliver's Travels by Jonathan Swift—written as an adult novel—is so popular with children that future editions are simplified.

1744

A Little Pretty Pocketbook is published by John Newbery, who believed that children should be entertained as they read.

1765

The Renowned History of Little Goody Two Shoes by Oliver Goldsmith is published; it is the first full-length children's novel.

1789

Songs of Innocence by William Blake introduces poetry to children.

1823

Grimm's Fairy Tales, by Wilhelm and Jacob Grimm, serves as the foundation for all versions of fairy tales that follow it, and represents the first time the traditional tales are put in print.

1843

A Christmas Carol by Charles Dickens entices both adults and children with its heartwarming theme.

1846

Fairy Tales by Hans Christian Andersen is not as "grim" a collection as Grimms' tales, and is widely embraced; *Book of Nonsense* by Edward Lear shows that silliness has a definite place in the world of children's books.

1865

Alice's Adventures in Wonderland by Lewis Carroll is considered the first great novel for children and the foundation of children's literature.

1867

Little Women by Louisa May Alcott proves that realistic stories with realistic characters can excite children.

1871

At the Back of the North Wind by George MacDonald continues the tradition of the fantasy story made popular by Lewis Carroll.

1876

The Adventures of Tom Sawyer by Mark Twain gives children a taste of "Americana" along with characters who aren't always good role models, but are a lot of fun.

1878

Under the Window by Kate Greenaway shows how well pictures and text can work together in books for the very young; her idealized view of childhood is a welcome if inaccurate interpretation.

1883

Treasure Island by Robert Louis Stevenson is widely lauded for its skilled plot structure and fully realized characters and setting.

1884

Heidi by Johanna Heusser Spyri is translated from German into English; it is embraced by children around the world who are drawn by Heidi's infectious enthusiasm for life.

1885

A Child's Garden of Verses by Robert Louis Stevenson is a collection of poems about childhood from a child's point of view.

1889

The Blue Fairy Book is a collection of tales from around the world edited by Andrew Lang; it is the first of twelve wildly popular fairy-tale collections, all designated by colors.

1894

The Jungle Book by Rudyard Kipling enthralls children with its daring young protagonist, Mowgli.

1899

The Story of the Treasure Seekers by Edith Nesbit will determine the direction of both the "family novel" and fantasy in the twentieth century; Edward Stratemeyer creates the first of more than sixty-five juvenile series with *The Rover Boys.*

1900

The Wizard of Oz by L. Frank Baum is considered the first American fairy tale.

1901

The Tale of Peter Rabbit by Beatrix Potter is the first great picture book success story.

1908

The Wind in the Willows by Kenneth Grahame is infused with a timeless sense of friendship and a love of nature.

1919

The Macmillan Publishing Company creates America's first children's book department; National Children's Book Week is established with the intention of celebrating and promoting children's books.

1921

The Newbery Medal is established to honor the finest American children's book of the year.

1922

Winnie-the-Pooh by A.A. Milne presents the last truly idyllic view of childhood with lighthearted prose and rhyme.

1924

The *Horn Book Magazine* is created, devoted entirely to the study of children's books.

1928

Millions of Cats by Wanda Gag takes picture books to a new level of creativity.

1930

The *Nancy Drew* series begins the same year Edward Strate-meyer dies, and is now overseen by his daughter, Harriet.

1932

Little House in the Big Woods by Laura Ingalls Wilder launches a hugely popular series based on the pioneer life of the author.

1937

The Hobbit by J.R.R. Tolkien embodies a world with its own rules and its own properties.

1938

The Caldecott Medal is created to honor the finest American picture book of the year.

1943

Johnny Tremain by Esther Forbes brings historical fiction to a child's reading level.

1947

Goodnight Moon by Margaret Wise Brown is the quintessential young child's first "bedtime story."

1950

The Lion, the Witch, and the Wardrobe by C.S. Lewis begins the seven-book *Chronicles of Narnia* series of allegorical fantasy.

1952

Anne Frank: Diary of a Young Girl demonstrates the power of a child's hopes and dreams for a future she never gets to experience; *Charlotte's Web* by E.B. White shows that the "animal story" is alive and well, and that children's literature can be as well written as any other genre.

1957

The Cat in the Hat by Dr. Seuss revolutionizes the way children are taught to read and ushers in the "easy-to-read" category.

1962

The Snowy Day by Ezra Jack Keats proves that a picture book story can be told very simply.

1963

Where the Wild Things Are by Maurice Sendak takes children on a wild ride into their innermost fears—and then brings them safely home.

1967

The Outsiders by S.E. Hinton heralds new realism in books for teenagers.

1970

Are You There, God? It's Me, Margaret by Judy Blume reveals the true pangs of adolescence.

1974

The Chocolate War by Robert Cormier tells older children that life doesn't always have a happy ending.

1977

Bridge to Terabithia by Katherine Paterson allows children to feel the grief of losing a loved one while learning how to heal.

1986

The Baby-Sitters Club by Ann M. Martin revives paperback series books for teenagers.

1993

Goosebumps by R.L. Stine brings the horror genre to the middle-grade reader.

1998

Harry Potter and the Sorcerer's Stone by J.K. Rowling breaks all publishing sales records and boosts the popularity of other fantasy novels.

For Further Research

Books

Marjorie N. Allen, *What Are Little Girls Made Of?* New York: FactsOnFile, 1999.

Robert Bator, ed., *Signposts to Criticism of Children's Literature.* Chicago: American Library Association, 1983.

Sandra L. Beckett, ed., *Reflections of Change: Children's Literature Since 1945.* Westport, CT: Greenwood Press, 1997.

Francelia Butler and Richard Rotert, eds., *Reflections on Literature for Children.* Hamden, CT: Library Professional Publication/Shoe String Press, 1984.

Francelia Butler and Richard Rotert, eds., *Triumphs of the Spirit in Children's Literature.* Hamden, CT: Library Professional Publication/Shoe String Press, 1986.

Marcus Crouch, *Treasure Seekers and Borrowers: Children's Books in Britain.* London: Library Association, 1962.

Sheila A. Egoff, G.T. Stubbs, and L.F. Ashley, eds., *Only Connect: Readings on Children's Literature,* 2nd edition. Canada: Oxford University Press, 1980.

Thomas Fensch, ed., *Of Sneetches and Whos and the Good Dr. Seuss: Essays on the Writings and Life of Theodor Geisel.* Jefferson, NC: McFarland, 1997.

Charles Frey and John Griffith, *The Literary Heritage of Childhood: An Appraisal of Children's Classics in the Western Tradition.* Westport, CT: Greenwood Press, 1987.

Jerry Griswold, *Audacious Kids: Coming of Age in America's Classic Children's Books.* New York: Oxford University Press, 1992.

James S. Jacobs and Michael O. Tunnell, *Children's Literature, Briefly.* Upper Saddle River, NJ: Prentice-Hall, 1996.

C.S. Lewis, *Letters to Children*. Eds. Lyle W. Dorsett and Marjorie Lamp Mead. New York: Macmillan, 1985.

Alison Lurie, *Don't Tell the Grown-ups: Subversive Children's Literature*. Boston: Little, Brown, 1990.

Margaret R. Marshall, *An Introduction to the World of Children's Books*. Great Britain: Gower, 1982.

Wendy Mass, *Great Authors of Children's Literature*. San Diego: Lucent Books, 2000.

Margaret Meek, Aidan Warlow, and Griselda Barton, *The Cool Web: The Pattern of Children's Reading*. London: The Bodley Head, 1977.

Cornelia Meigs, ed., *A Critical History of Children's Literature*, Revised Edition. New York: Macmillan, 1969.

Maurice Sendak, *Caldicott and Co.: Notes on Books and Pictures*. New York: Farrar, Straus and Giroux, 1988.

Anita Silvey, *Children's Books and Their Creators*. New York: Houghton Mifflin, 1995.

Ann Thwaite, *The Brilliant Career of Winnie-the-Pooh*. New York: Dutton's Children's Books, 1994.

John Rowe Townsend, *Twentieth Century Children's Literature*. Chicago: St. James Press, 1989.

Mark I. West, *Trust Your Children: Voices Against Censorship in Children's Literature*. New York: Neal-Schuman, 1988.

Jackie Wullschlager, *Inventing Wonderland*. New York: Free Press, 1995.

PERIODICALS AND NEWSPAPERS

Barbara Bader, "American Picture Books: From Max's Metaphorical Monsters to Lilly's Purple Plastic Purse," *Horn Book Magazine*, vol. LXXIV, no. 2, March/April 1998.

Olivia Barker, "Popularity of 'Potter' Stirs Cauldron of Dissent: Books' Foes Cite Rights of Parents, Free Speech," *USA Today*, December 28, 1999.

Meredeth Eliassen, "From Dime Novels to Disney: San Francisco's Archer Collection Houses It All," *School Library Journal*, July 1995.

Adam Gopnik, "Grim Fairy Tales," *New Yorker*, November 18, 1996.

Alan Jacobs, "*Harry Potter*'s Magic," *First Things*, January 2000.

Stefan Kanfer, "Read 'Em and Weep," *Men's Health*, March 2000.

Katherine Kersten, "These Books Induce Fear While Driving Out Pity: R.L. Stine's 'Shock Fiction' Comes with a Price," *Minneapolis Star Tribune*, January 29, 1997.

Palm Beach Post, "Thank You, Harry Potter!" March 12, 2000.

Martha V. Parravano, "'Alive and Vigorous': Questioning the Newbery," *Horn Book Magazine*, July/August 1999.

Paula Poundstone, "Tales from the Crib," *Mother Jones*, May/June 1997.

Pamela Protheroe, "Are Picture Books Harmful?" *New Scientist*, June 19, 1993.

Susan Stan, "Going Global: World Literature for American Children," *Theory into Practice*, vol. 38, no. 3, Summer 1999.

Roger Sutton, "Lights Out?" *Horn Book Magazine*, January 11, 1998.

INDEX